For Your Freedom and Ours

For Your Freedom and Ours

The Polish Armed Forces in the Second World War

Margaret Brodniewicz-Stawicki

Vanwell Publishing Limited
St. Catharines, Ontario

Vanwell publishing acknowledges the financial support of the Government of Canada though the Book Publishing Industry Development Program for our publishing activities.

Cover and book design,
maps and illustrations: Margaret Brodniewicz-Stawicki

Vanwell Publishing Limited
1 Northrup Crescent
P.O. Box 2131
St. Catharines, Ontario L2R 7S2

P.O. Box 1207
Lewiston, New York
U.S.A. 14092

Printed in Canada

Canadian Cataloguing in Publication Data

Brodniewicz-Stawicki, Margaret
    For your freedom and ours : the Polish armed forces in the Second World War

Includes bibliographical references and index.
ISBN 1-55125-035-7

1. Poland — Armed Forces — History — World War, 1939-1945. 2. Poland — Armed Forces — History — World War, 1939-1945 — Pictorial works.
3. World War, 1939-1945 — Poland. 4. World War, 1939-1945 — Poland — Pictorial works. I. Title.

D765.B76 1999   940.54'09438   C99-932000-9

Contents

39

91

111

167

Acknowledgements

I would like to acknowledge the Polish Combatants Association in Canada for its invaluable contribution, support and consultation, and for its help, without which this book would not have happened.

My very special thanks to Mieczyslaw Szczecinski, former prisoner of Kozielsk, veteran of the battle of Monte Cassino, for his patience in finding answers to all of my questions, and to Marian Fijal, Elizabeth Rogacki, Richard Rogacki and Henryk Starczewski for their inspiration, enthusiasm and the assistance that led to this book.

■ ■ ■

I would like to thank the organizations and individuals who kindly allowed me to use their resources: The Polish Consulate in Toronto, for allowing me to reproduce the photographs from the exhibit about *Polish Armies In The Second World War*; Stefan S. Baluk, author of *Poles On The Front Of World War II*; Stanislaw Kopf, author of *Lata Okupacji*, and Lucjan Krolikowski, author of *Stolen Childhood,* for their permission to reproduce parts from their works; to the Sikorski Museum and Andrzej Suchcic, for help and guidance through their archives; and to all the veterans and their families who provided me with access to their private photo albums and war memoirs — Krzysztof Ciuk, Danusia Figiel, Marian Fijal, Jan Gasztold, Elizabeth Getlich, Tola and Kazimierz Grabowski, Zdzislawa Lempicki, Aleksandra Markiewicz, Stanislawa Onoszko, Henryk Starczewski, Mieczyslaw Szczecinski, Jerzy Tomaszewski, Jan Towarnicki, and Waclaw Zankowicz.

■ ■ ■

I am grateful to my dear friend Shelley Robertson for her priceless help and to my family — my husband, Andrew, for his photo editing assistance; to my three beloved children, Agatha, Agnes and Michael, for their great support and help and for not complaining for lack of family life during my work on this project; and to my parents and my brother for their enthusiasm and encouragement.

■ ■ ■

I would also like to thank Angela Dobler, Jan Fedorowicz, Nick Harris, Ben Kooter, the publishing crew, for their endless spark and vitality, which have been a special inspiration to me.

Foreword

The last full-scale battle of the Polish Campaign was fought at Kock (north of Lublin) on October 5, 1939. The battle of Kock ended five weeks of struggle against an enemy that was superior in equipment and personnel, and that enjoyed a stronger strategic position as well as the advantage of operational initiative. Moreover, any further organized defence of Poland was rendered impossible by a sudden Soviet attack on her unprotected Eastern frontier in the third week of the German offensive.

Despite these sudden and cataclysmic setbacks, the Polish nation refused to admit that the war was over. While regular military operations on Polish soil came to an end, resistance continued underground and it went on in foreign lands, by the side of Poland's Allies. Polish officers and enlisted soldiers risked their lives to cross the so-called "green frontiers" into Rumania and Hungary, from where they made their way to France, where a new Polish Army was being organized, or to Great Britain, Africa, and the Middle East.

On several occasions during the Second World War, Polish armed forces decisively influenced the course of the struggle. Even the doomed campaign of September 1939 gave their allies valuable breathing time in which to mobilize their resources and prepare for battle.

During the Battle of Britain, Polish fighters scored an above-average number of "kills" against the Luftwaffe, making it probable that their contribution was vital to turning the tide of the air war.

Later, Polish land forces took a prominent part in the capture of Monte Cassino, which opened the road to Rome. They also closed the Falaise Gap, an action that prevented German units from retreating from Normandy and thus sealed the success of the D-Day invasion.

As the first country to be attacked by Germany, Poland was in the war longer than any of its Allies. During these long years, the fighting qualities of its soldiers were demonstrated time and again. They fought so long and so gallantly because they were animated by a deep and passionate patriotism, because they were determined to restore freedom and independence to their country and because they believed in the ideals of liberty, justice and right, for which both they and their Allies went to war.

For Poland, the Second World War lasted five years, eight months and eight days. During that time, Poland lost 6,000,000 citizens and thirty-eight per cent of her national property. The graves of Poland's soldiers and partisans are scattered over all the battlefields of this conflict.

Despite the country's losses, Polish resistance did not abate. In May of 1945, the Polish Armed Forces had about 600,000 officers and men under arms. This made Poland the fourth largest contributor to the war effort after the Soviet Union, the United States and Great Britain.

The Poles played a prominent role at Narvik, in France, in the Battle of Britain, in Libya and Italy, on the Murmansk run, in Normandy and at Arnhem. In the end, there was no significant action of the Second World War that did not involve Polish participation.

IX

Der Oberste Befehlshaber der Wehrmacht   Berlin, den 31.8 39.

OKW/WFA Nr. 170 /39 g.K.Chefs. L I

8 Ausfertigungen
2. Ausfertigung.

Geheime Kommandosache

Chef Sache
Nur durch Offizier

Weisung Nr. 1

für die Kriegführung.

1.) Nachdem alle politischen Möglichkeiten erschöpft sind, um auf friedlichem Wege eine für Deutschland unerträgliche Lage an seiner Ostgrenze zu beseitigen, habe ich mich zur gewaltsamen Lösung entschlossen.

2.) Der Angriff gegen Polen ist nach den für Fall Weiss getroffenen Vorbereitungen zu führen mit den Abänderungen, die sich beim Heer durch den inzwischen fast vollendeten Aufmarsch ergeben.

Aufgabenverteilung und Operationsziel bleiben unverändert.

Angriffstag: 1.9.39.

Angriffszeit ....

Diese Zeit gilt auch für die Unternehmungen Gdingen - Danziger Bucht und Brücke Dirschau.

zunutzen. Angriffe gegen London bleiben meiner Entscheidung vorbehalten.

Die Angriffe gegen das engl. Mutterland sind unter dem Gesichtspunkt vorzubereiten, dass unzureichender Erfolg mit Teilkräften unter allen Umständen zu vermeiden ist.

X

The Supreme Commander of The Armed Forces   Berlin 31.8.39

Directive No.1   8 copies

for the conduct of war   2nd copy

1.) All political possibilities having been exhausted in attempts by peaceful means to overcome a position which has become intolerable for Germany on its eastern borders, I have decided on the violent solution.

2.) The attack on Poland is to be conducted in accordance with the preparations drawn-up for Case White, incorporating the changes resulting from the almost completed mobilisation of the Army which has taken place in the meantime.

Appointment of duties and aim of the operation are unchanged

Date of attack: 1.9.39

Time of attack:.................

This time also applies to the operations around Gdingen-Bay of Danzing and the Dirschau bridge.............

.... exploited. Any decision to attack London resides with me.

Preparations for the attacks against the English homeland should be made bearing in mind that limited success through a failure to fully commit one's forces is something to be avoided under any circumstances.

Signed Adolf Hitler

"First, Poland had been again overrun by two of the great Powers which held her in bondage for 150 years, but were unable to quench the spirit of the Polish nation. The heroic defence of Warsaw shows that the soul of Poland is indestructible, and that she will rise again like a rock, which may for a spell be submerged by a tidal wave, but which remains a rock.

But everything that is happening to the Czechs pales in comparison with the atrocities which as I speak here this afternoon are being perpetrated upon the Poles. In German-occupied Poland the most hideous form of terrorism prevails. In this there are two distinct phases. In the first the Germans tried to cow the population by shooting individuals picked at random from the towns. At one place where they had decided to shoot thirty-five people they collected thirty-four, and then, finding themselves one short, went into a chemist's shop and seized the first person they saw to make up the tally.

But later on they became more discriminating — they made careful search for the natural leaders of Polish life: the nobles, the landowners, the priests, as well as prominent workmen and peasants. It is estimated that upwards of fifteen thousand intellectual leaders have been shot. These horrible mass executions are a frequent occurrence. At one place three hundred were lined up against the wall; at another a group of drunken German officers are said to have shot seventy hostages in prison; at another a hundred and thirty-six Polish students, some of whom were only twelve or thirteen years old, were butchered. Torture has been used. Press gangs seize men and women in the streets and drive them off in droves to forced labour in Germany."

Speech of Prime Minister Winston S. Churchill on the BBC on October 1, 1939, *The Churchill War Papers,* Volume 1, *At The Admiralty, in September 1939-May 1940,* by Martin Gilbert

Poland

POLAND

"Wartime in Poland lasted longer than for any other country in Europe (except Germany). Between the commencement of the Nazi attack at dawn on September 1st, 1939 and the final capitulation of the Nazi Reich on VE Day, May 9, 1945, there stretched over two thousand days of violence and suffering. In proportion to its size, Poland incurred far more damage and casualties than any country on earth."

Norman Davies in *Heart Of Europe — A Short History Of Poland*

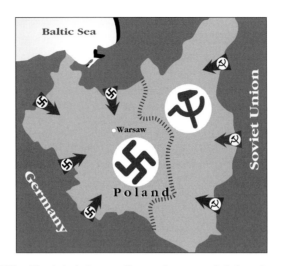

On September 1, 1939, without declaring war, Germany's army and air force invaded Poland from the north, west and south. Then, 16 days later, on September 17, the Soviet Union attacked from the east. For all Europe, the Nazi invasion marked the beginning of the Second World War. For Poland, the Soviet invasion marked the beginning of a 50-year-long struggle against communism.

German soldiers break through the border in The Sopot-Gdynia (Danzing) area.

14

German soldiers take a break in northwest Poland during their advances to East Prussia. The German army, or "Wehrmacht," evacuated thousands of innocent civilians in a vain attempt to terrorize the Polish people into submission.

In August 1939, Hitler and Stalin made a shameful pact to dismember Poland. Hitler did not believe England and France would intervene, because they had allowed him to swallow up Czechoslovakia the previous year. He hoped the Poles would simply submit to the overwhelming power of Nazi Germany.

But the Poles had recovered their independence only in 1918, after more than a century of occupation by the empires of Russia, Prussia and Austria. They were prepared to make any sacrifice to preserve their freedom.

When the Germans attacked, Poland was subjected to the first use of the Blitzkrieg. It was over in six weeks. Even so, the Poles did inflict damage on the German army. Almost 90,000 German soldiers were killed or wounded, far more than in the eight-week war in France the following spring; a huge number of armoured vehicles and other equipment was destroyed; and the German Air Force lost more than 400 aircraft, a rate of loss that was never again exceeded, except for a few weeks during the Battle of Britain.

On September 17, when they were certain Polish resistance was crumbling, the Soviets invaded Poland from the east. Because all of Poland's Armed Forces were fighting against Germany, there was little opposition to the Red Army.

The German battleship *Schleswig-Holstein* on a courtesy visit to Gdansk. At dawn on
September 1, 1939, when German aircraft indiscriminately bombed Polish cities, the visiting
battleship opened fire on the Polish garrison on Westerplatte Island.

Westerplatte's stubborn defence.
The Garrison on Westerplatte guarded the entrance to the Gdansk harbour. During the attack it was shelled by
the battleship *Schleswig-Holstein*, two torpedo boats, *Von der Groeben* and *T-196,* and artillery. After seven
days of heroic defence, Westerplatte surrendered. When Germans entered the ruins, they found almost all of
the defenders dead or wounded.

Left: The Polish PZL-37 was one of the most technologically advanced medium bombers in the world. Poland's total number of aircraft in 1939 was 36.
Centre: An anti-aircraft platoon. Right: The battlefield in Bory Tucholskie, where the Polish army "Pomerania" was defeated.

After

Poland's collapse, Polish soldiers and young men sought to escape enemy internment camps and to reach France, where a new Polish army was being organized. First, they had to reach Rumania and Hungary. Under a treaty with Rumania, certain ministries and the Diplomatic Corps were allowed to proceed to Rumania as early as September 5, 1939. The road led to Kuty on the Polish-Rumanian border, and then south to Bucharest.

After the Russian invasion on September 17, 1939, the Kuty sector was occupied by Bolshevik soldiers and escape became almost impossible. Later, when Germans occupied all of Poland's territory, only the bravest and the luckiest succeeded in getting away.

Poles smuggled themselves across the border. They crossed open, unprotected fields or the snowy passes of the High Tatra and Carpathian mountains. Although the Rumanian and Hungarian populations were generous in their welcome, the authorities, by contrast, flung many of these Polish arrivals into internment camps. In many cases, bribery was the only way out and it was not uncommon for Poles to reach France with nothing. There, they joined the Polish army being formed under the command of General Wladyslaw Sikorski. More than 12,000 men crossed into France this way and were sent immediately to assembly points in the southern part of the country.

Other Poles who managed to escape by way of Rumania or Hungary went to Palestine and Egypt and were later incorporated into the Polish Army under the command of General Stanislaw Kopanski.

For the Poles who made their way into Lithuania or Latvia, further escape was virtually impossible. Russia soon occupied these two countries and only a few individuals managed to go to Britain via the Baltic Sea or the Scandinavian countries.

Those Poles who found themselves under Russian occupation were treated no better than those in the German sector. Intellectuals, politicians, professionals, members of the military and priests of the church, together with their families, were herded together and driven into Russia's vast territories to be placed in the labour camps and prisons of the Far East, Siberia or Central Asia. They were forced to live under the greatest misery and degradation. Exactly how many died we will never know.

The Polish Cavalry formed part of light and heavy artillery units and anti-tank artillery units. In defensive battles against German aggressors, it fought famous battles along the Bzura River in the Kutno area and then, in the last regular battle of the September campaign, the Battle of Kock. General Kleeberg, the commander of the operational group *Polesie,* which fought the Battle of Kock, said after capitulation:
"I know that you will turn out again if necessary. Poland is not yet dead!"

Execution of peasants by the military police and SS in a village.
Before and after execution.

"In the Polish campaign, the soldiers had been left to fight the war while the Action Groups — the Einsatzgruppen — followed in their wake to attend to the civilian population. For the first year, the Jews were brutalized, but far more Christians than Jewish Poles were killed — a fact rarely acknowledged by either historians or the media."

Gitta Sereny in *Albert Speer: His Battle With Truth*

The Germans believed that the public hanging of patriots would break the resistance of the Polish people.

19

"The Germans shot 20,000 civilian hostages in Bydgoszcz alone....

In the Extraordinary Pacification Campaign of 1940 some 15,000 Polish priests, teachers and political leaders were transported to Dachau or shot in the Palmiry Forest. The first experiments were made in euthanasia, in the selection of children for racial breeding, in slave-labour schemes, and in gas chambers.

At the same time, Soviet (NKVD) terror in many ways exceeded that of the Nazis. The NKVD followed guide-lines based on their own idea of class analysis, assigning some two million people associated with the professions or with pre-war state employment to forcible deportation.

Each side was working with equal vigour for the reduction of the Poles to the condition of a leaderless, friendless nation."

Norman Davies in *Heart Of Europe — A Short History Of Poland*

Top: Polish prisoners of war are interrogated by German soldiers. They were asked to take off their jackets to make them look like civilians.

Left: German soldiers stand over the bodies of murdered prisoners of war. Ciepelow, September 8, 1939

Top, left and right: The humiliation of Jews became the SS soldier's favourite pastime.
Bottom left: Punishment for participating in a Catholic mass. More than 2,300 Catholic clergy were killed in prisons and camps.
Bottom right: Execution of Polish people in Ustronie Slaskie, 1940. *Jerzy Tomaszewski*

*Children suffered and faced
an unsure future*

Partisans did not accept capitulation

Clockwise from top left: A forest unit in Stanislawow District, August 1944; the Home Army 6th Independent Partisan Brigade marches out for a reconnaissance operation; a commander of a special "Diversion Unit" examines a mine before blowing up a railway bridge near Pogorzne, April 5, 1944. *Sikorski Museum;*
A German-damaged train on the Eastern front.

"We know the story of the Polish underground movement, unrivaled by any underground movement in any part of Europe...."

Sir Percy Harris speaking in the House of Commons during debate on the Crimea Conference. February 28, 1945

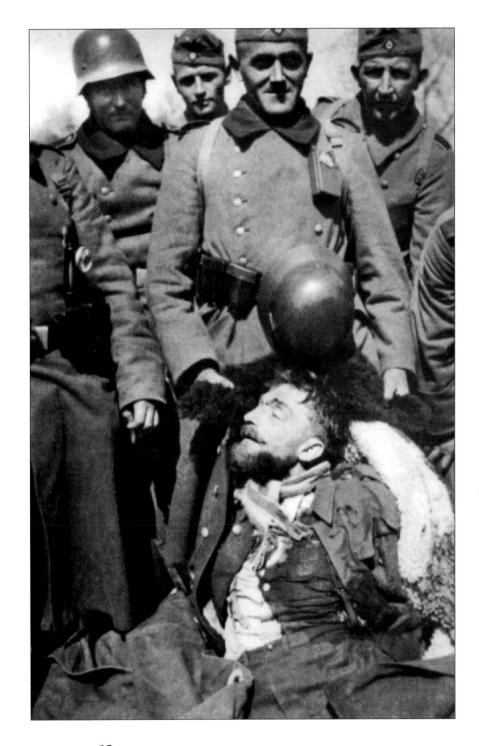

Legendary "Hubal" — Major Henryk Dobrzanski — did not accept the capitulation and started successful guerrilla operations with his unit. In a battle fought against the Wehrmacht expedition on April 30, 1940, the commander of Hubal's soldiers was killed. His body was buried by Germans and his grave was never found.

German Extermination Camps in Occupied Poland

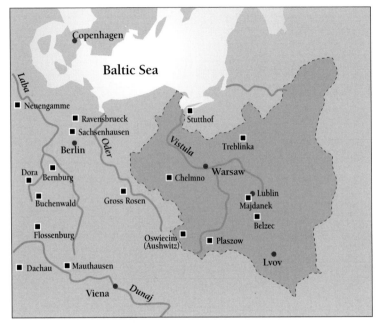

Location of major extermination camps.

The meticulously prepared Nazi program to exterminate subjugated nations was chiefly based on extermination camps. The Germans randomly snatched innocent civilians off the streets and sent them to the camps. Anyone remotely suspected of helping the partisans, or dealing on the black market, or hiding their Jewish neighbours, was also sent to the camps — often with their whole family.

More than ninety per cent of the ancient and vigorous Jewish community — the largest in the world — was indiscriminately and cruelly murdered in these death factories.

There were more than 2,000 camps and sub-camps on Polish territory, in which perished Jewish, Catholic and Orthodox Poles, Jews from other countries, and victims from other nationalities in Nazi-conquered Europe. Small children, elders, the weak and the ill were immediately murdered as not useful for work.

Of these appalling death factories, undoubtedly the worst were Auschwitz, Stuthoff, Gross Rosen, Majdanek, Chelmno, Sobibor and Treblinka.

The Nazi system of genocide was the most cruel in the history of mankind.

Disturbingly, the Nazi program of extermination was not just the work of a small gang of criminal bigots. A number of ordinary, civilized Germans, as well as people of other origins, aided and abetted the Nazis in committing their unspeakable crimes.

Prisoners in Auschwitz. Their working shift was eleven hours. Those too weak and ill to work were murdered.

A crematorium.
It could incinerate 5,000 bodies in twenty-four hours.

27

Warsaw Ghetto

The population of the Warsaw Ghetto in one of its squares. Their
property was confiscated, and by a decree of March 4, 1941, the Jews, together
with Gypsies, were deprived of any legal protection and were declared criminals.

More than 600,000 Jews from all parts of Poland were herded into the Warsaw Ghetto. Any contact with people from the Ghetto was strictly forbidden, and anyone going in or out was shot.

On November 10, 1941, the governor of the Warsaw District, Dr. Fischer, announced the death penalty for any Jew who tried to leave the Ghetto as well as for anyone who helped Jews by providing them with shelter, food, or transportation of any kind.

To help the Jews who escaped from the Ghetto, the Polish underground movement organized a special group, called "Zegota." For Jews lucky enough to escape the Ghetto, Zegota's members provided shelter, some financial support and false documents. Altogether, some 40,000 Jews went into hiding throughout Poland, 20,000 of them in Warsaw alone. These numbers do not include those Jews who were found by the Germans and, together with the families helping them, were shot dead or sent to extermination camps.

Starting in 1941, small groups were transported by rail to extermination camps in Belzec, Majdanek and Treblinka. From the beginning, they were told they were just being relocated to work in factories.

The first information about the true plight of the Jews in Poland reached London in the middle of 1942. Thereafter, a steady stream of documentation, including photographs, was forwarded to the Polish Government-in-Exile. The Polish Government immediately informed other countries about the crimes being committed against the Jews. The truth was so appalling and hard to believe that it was initially met with silence, not only from England and the United States, but also from prominent Jewish communities.

Children of
the Warsaw Ghetto

30

Little child of war
Alone and terrified
Crying to the world
A world that did not hear.

Little child of war
Buried, long forgotten
In an unknown grave
No-one shed a tear.

Little child of war
Whose picture brings
Anguish even now
It's more than I can bear.

Little child of war
I too am one with you
I care.

Author unknown.

Found pinned to the photographic display
"For Your Freedom and Ours,"
Toronto City Hall, November 11, 1994

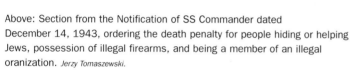

35. LESZCZYŃSKI MICHAŁ, z Rudy Sieleckiej, z powodu nieuprawnionego posiadania broni,

36. KALINIEWICZ WASYL, z Łanów Polskich, z powodu nieuprawnionego posiadania broni,,

37. IRZEK JULIA, z Lemberg, z powodu ukrywania żydów,

38. MALAWSKA ur. WILCZYŃSKA WIKTORIA, z Lemberg, z powodu ukrywania żydów,

39. ŚLADOWSKA HALINA, ur. KRZYMIENIEWSKA, z Lemberg, z powodu ukrywania żydów,

40. JOSEFEK MARIA, ur. SLOWICZ, z Lemberg, z powodu ukrywania żydów,

41. JOSEFEK BRONISŁAW, z Lemberg, z powodu ukrywania żydów,

42. STELMASZCZUK JERZY, z Hoholów, z powodu nieuprawnionego posiadania broni,

43. HALICKI ROMAN, z Warszawy, z powodu udziału w zakazanych organizacjach i nieuprawnionego posiadania broni,

44. PUKAS EDWARD, z Lemberg, z powodu udziału w zakazanych organizacjach,

Above: Section from the Notification of SS Commander dated December 14, 1943, ordering the death penalty for people hiding or helping Jews, possession of illegal firearms, and being a member of an illegal oranization. *Jerzy Tomaszewski.*

Right, top and bottom: Warsaw Ghetto, 1941. Food smuggled from the "Aryan" side was an important factor in survival. *Jerzy Tomaszewski*

"It is often asked why so little help was extended to Polish Jewry in the hour of its distress. The question can only be put by people with no conception of the circumstances in occupied Poland, which bore little relation to the relatively genteel condition of occupied Denmark, France, or Holland. The Polish population at large lived under the formal threat of instant execution for the entire family of anyone found sheltering, feeding, or helping Jews. In this light, it is as pointless to ask why the Poles did little to help the Jews as to enquire why the Jews did nothing to assist the Poles."

Norman Davies in *Heart Of Europe, A Short History Of Poland*

32

Ghetto Uprising

The Germans did not spare the last survivors of the uprising.

In December 1942, the Jews in the Ghetto retaliated for their treatment. Resistance was focused on a group known as the Jewish Fighting Union, which received some assistance from Polish armed organizations outside the Ghetto as well as from the Supreme Command of the Polish Home Army and The People's Guard. When, in January of 1943, the Nazis made their first attempt to liquidate the Ghetto, they met with unexpected resistance and were forced to withdraw.

A new and better-prepared German offensive involving more than 2,000 SS, Wehrmacht, and police started at 6 a.m. on April 19, 1943. The Germans treated the fighting in the Ghetto as a regular military operation in which they engaged mortars and artillery. Their ultimatum demanding surrender was rejected and fighting continued both day and night.

The Jews of the Ghetto fought under the command of the twenty-four-year-old Mordechaj Anielewicz. In this unequal struggle, victory was impossible, but in demonstrating their heroic determination, the defenders of the Ghetto sent a message to the ages.

On the night of April 21, the Germans began setting fires in the Ghetto with the objective of burning out the defenders, house by house and street by street.

On May 5, 1943, in a radio speech, General Wladyslaw Sikorski spoke to the world about the crimes being committed against the people of the Warsaw Ghetto. Three days later, Mordechaj Anielewicz and the other leaders of the Jewish Fighting Union committed suicide. In solidarity, Szmul Zygielbojm, a member of the Polish National Council in London, committed suicide on May 11, 1943, as a protest against the silence of the world about the Ghetto and about the plight of the Jews under Nazi occupation.

He stated in his letter:

"By my death I want to express my protest against the passivity of the world, which looks upon and permits the extermination of the Jewish nation."

By May 16, the last pockets of resistance succumbed as the Germans shot the Ghetto's remaining defenders.
Of the Ghetto's 600,000 inhabitants, 14,000 died during the fighting or were burned alive in their houses and 7,000 were murdered in the death camp at Treblinka. The rest were taken to Majdanek, where almost all perished.

The uprising in the Warsaw Ghetto showed that Poland's Jews would not go meekly to their death. A handful of young men and women, armed with hand-guns, grenades, and home-made bomb launchers, held a brigade of SS infantrymen at bay for three weeks. It was the largest single act of resistance to occur in Poland until the outbreak of the Warsaw Uprising fifteen months later.

April 25, 1943, Easter Sunday. The Nazis began their murderous operation at 1 p.m.

The Germans started enormous fires that forced the Jews to leave their hiding places. Many were buried alive or burned to death. Not one of those captured was spared.

34

Women fighters of the Ghetto uprising await their fate.

Enormous fires force the Jews to leave their shelters and hiding places.
Gestapo chief Heinrich Himmler ordered the Warsaw Ghetto totally destroyed. The chief of the SS and of the police of the Warsaw district, Jungen Stroop, was a commander of this operation. On his special order, captured rabbis were killed on the spot.

Oswiecim (Auschwitz) camp. When the crematorium fell behind in its work, the murdered were burned in the open.

Members of the Polish Home Army who escaped from the Old City section of Warsaw after its capitulation. The picture was taken on Warecka Street.
At centre, Zofia Darowska, code-named "Zoska." She was killed a few days after this picture was taken. *Jerzy Tomaszewski*
They all believed help would come soon. The Soviet Red Army, standing nearby, not only did not help but the Bolsheviks developed anti-uprising propaganda.
The partisans' units and soldiers, as well as civilians from territories liberated from German occupation trying to reach Warsaw to assist the uprising, were disarmed, interned and deported.

The Warsaw Uprising

German soldiers taken prisoner by the Home Army. *Jerzy Tomaszewski*

Poland fought in isolation through five years of occupation in the hope that aid would come. The Polish underground resistance organized the Home Army almost from the beginning of the war. In fact, the Home Army's units were operating even before the Germans had established their police and administrative machine in Warsaw. Because Poland occupied a key position for transports passing from Russia to Germany and later from Germany to Russia, the Home Army was determined to do everything it could to prevent reserves and supplies from reaching their destination. In terms of resistance to German occupation, the actions of Poland's Home Army were among the most effective resistance to be found anywhere in Europe.

A military command structure for the Home Army came into existence in 1940 under the name of the Leading Military Organizations of Underground Poland. A single unified military organization — the Home Army — evolved by 1942. After that time, there was even an underground Parliament, an underground administration of justice and an army that consisted of half a million people, of whom 100,000 were women. By the end of the war, the commander of the Home Army reported directly to the commander-in-chief of all Polish forces and the Polish Government-in-Exile in London.

In the summer of 1944, as the Red Army was nearing the Vistula River, representatives of the Polish government in London and the Home Army called for military action against the Nazis in Warsaw. On August 1, at 5 p.m., an insurrection broke out in the city. General Tadeusz Bor-Komorowski initiated the uprising by issuing the code word "Burza" (Storm).

The objectives of the uprising were to accelerate the defeat of the Germans, help the approaching Allied armies, and establish strong civilian authorities on liberated territory. Armed with weapons made in secret workshops and stolen German equipment, the defenders waged an uneven conflict, believing

Barricade on Chmielna Street, August 1944

they would be relieved by the Soviets, who were less than twenty kilometres away. A large part of the city was liberated but Warsaw's defenders had ammunition for only seven days.

On August 3, 1944, Stalin promised the premier of the Polish Government-in-Exile, S. Mikolajczyk, that the Red Army would attack the Germans if the Warsaw Uprising lasted for at least six days. In the end, the uprising continued for sixty-three days but the promised Russian support never came.

The Soviets were not interested in helping the Poles, whom they considered ideological enemies. Soviet Premier Josef Stalin intended to dominate Poland and was not willing to help an independent Polish authority establish itself. Instead, the Russians stood by on the other side of the Vistula and watched the Germans obliterate Warsaw. Unwilling to act themselves, the Soviets even refused Allied aid missions permission to land at fields in the eastern parts of Polish territory that they had already liberated from German occupation.

Severely under-equipped, the Warsaw garrison fought on for two months. More than 20,000 Polish soldiers were killed, as were hundreds of thousands of civilians, murdered by the Germans during the uprising, or shipped off to Auschwitz after the garrison surrendered. The Germans destroyed most of the city during the fighting, and on Hitler's personal orders later burned whatever buildings remained.

A courier from Scout Unit distributes the partisans' news bulletin. *Jerzy Tomaszewski*

41

On Warecka Street, defenders of the Old City feel safe again. *Jerzy Tomaszewski*

"For our part we salute the heroes of Warsaw, accord them our deep admiration, and trust that even at this late hour the Allied leaders will give them the little help that stands between victory of the people of Warsaw and destruction so near to their hour of liberation...."

Article in the weekly *Tribune* on the Warsaw Uprising, August 11, 1944

A building on Napoleon Square is blown up. *S. Braun, Historic Museum of Warsaw*

A Polish soldier defends a barricade along the only passage between the south and north-of-central section of the city. The Germans destroyed it during the day and Polish soldiers rebuilt it during the night. *Jerzy Tomaszewski*

Partisans at a post keep German tanks from entering Nowy Swiat Street. *Jerzy Tomaszewski*

Men in the "Rafal" group fought until capitulation of the Powisle section of the city. At right is a courier, Andrzej Tomaszewski — brother of the photographer. *Jerzy Tomaszewski*

45

Meeting in front of the Prudential Building on Napoleon Square.
S. Braun, Historical Museum of Warsaw

"To complete the picture, though it has nothing to do with the efforts being made in Italy, it should be added that in the meantime the Polish Prime Minister Mr. Mikolajczyk, who was in Moscow, appealed to Marshal Stalin for help from the Russian side. This help was apparently promised, and Mr. Mikolajczyk sent a telegram from Moscow through British diplomatic channels on August 9th with details of what Marshal Stalin had promised him and instructions for the VI Bureau to send on to the Commander in Chief in Warsaw for contacting the Russian Commander across the Vistula. These efforts were ineffective, and in spite of a joint appeal to Mr. Molotov by the British and American Ambassadors in Moscow on August 18, an approach which was met by denials of the value of Polish resistance in Warsaw and wholesale condemnation of the Polish Government for causing it, no Russian help was sent to Warsaw until the night of September 13."

From the papers of Lieutenant Colonel H.M. Threlfall, Commander Force 139, Special operations to Poland, from the Mediterranean theatre of operation. May 30, 1945. *IWM*

"The message from you and Mr. Churchill about Warsaw has reached me. I should like to state my views.
Sooner or later the truth about the handful of power-seeking criminals who launched the Warsaw adventure will out.
Those elements, playing on the credulity of the inhabitants of Warsaw, exposed practically unarmed
people to German guns, armour and aircraft."

Letter from Soviet Premier Josef Stalin to U.S. President Franklin D. Roosevelt and British Prime Minister Winston Churchill dated September 4, 1944, in *The Secret History of World War II*

Young partisans. *Jerzy Tomaszewski.*

The commander of the German 9th Army assigned to fight against the Warsaw Uprising was SS Obergruppenfuhrer General Erich von dem Bach.
The Germans called for additional SS troops and police units, which totalled, with the 9th Army, more than 50,000 soldiers.

War trophy. A captured Nazi truck with "Warsaw 1944" painted on it was used to distribute food among partisan groups. *Jerzy Tomaszewski*

War trophy. Major A. Kotowski — "Okon" — shows off a Nazi flag captured during the fight in Wola.

A group of couriers — "sewer travellers."

Storm sewers were the only connection between the Mokotow part of the city and the city centre. They were frequently used by couriers and partisans.

In September, after the capitulation of the Old City, Germans discovered the sewer system as a means of escape for partisans. They put gasoline inside the drains and set it on fire. They placed grenades and bombs at entrances to sewers, killing hundreds of young boys and girls.

Coming out of a sewer.

Preparing so-called "Molotov Cocktails" — bottles filled with butane gas — from a captured German car to throw at German tanks.

"The fight of the people of Warsaw, which has now continued for four long weeks against overwhelming odds and under the most appalling conditions, will undoubtedly go down in history as one of the outstanding features of this war, not only because of its heroism but also as evidence of the determination of the Polish Nation to exterminate the common enemy and to gain the independence they so richly deserve."

Letter from Lord Roundell Selborne, minister of Economic Warfare, to the Polish General Staff, September 4, 1944

51

Collecting the dead after a heavy artillery attack. *Jerzy Tomaszewski*

"I am sure I am expressing the feelings of the House, as well as those of His Majesty's Government, in paying tribute to the heroic stand of the Polish Home Army and the civilian population of Warsaw. Their resistance to overwhelming odds, under inconceivable conditions and hardship, came to an end on October 2nd, after a fight which lasted 63 days.

The final fall of Warsaw, at a time when the Allied armies are everywhere victorious and when the final defeat of Germany is in sight, must come as a very bitter blow to all Poles. At such a moment I wish to express our respect for all Poles who fell and suffered at Warsaw, our sympathy with the Polish nation in this further grievous loss. Our confidence that the days of her tribulation are rapidly drawing to an end is unshakable.

When the final Allied victory is achieved, the epic of Warsaw will not be forgotten. It will remain a deathless memory for Poles and for the friends of freedom all over the world."

Statement in the House of Commons by Prime Minister Winston Churchill on the fate of Warsaw. October 5, 1944

A cross on the graves of wounded partisans who were burned alive on September 2, 1944, in a basement of the house at 25 Podwale Street.

"There is no doubt that the Russians suffered a defeat to the east of Warsaw (two armoured divisions were said to be lost), but not a defeat strong enough to halt a whole Soviet army for nearly half a year. Whatever the Russians' reasons, which have never been fully explained, it is certain that the Polish resistance led by the gallant if rash Bor-Komorowski was successfully crushed by the Germans during this five-month delay."

Brian Gardner in *The Wasted Hour — The Tragedy Of 1945*

Civilians suffered great losses — 180,000 were killed or died from wounds.

This picture was taken after capitulation. Civilians, on Gestapo chief Heinrich Himmler's orders, were forced to leave the ruins of the city. They were allowed to take only hand luggage with them.

S.Braun, Historic Museum of Warsaw

"All that should be remembered is that the garrison and its commander, who is now a prisoner in German hands, fought against the common enemy with a noble tenacity worthy of their cause and of their race, and have put all Allies deeper in Poland's debt."

The Daily Telegraph, article headlined "Epitaph" on the fall of Warsaw, October 6, 1944

Top: After handing over weapons. Eleven thousand and sixty-eight soldiers, including five generals, were taken prisoner. Representatives of the Home Army signed the capitulation act on October 2, 1944. Eighteen thousand insurgents were killed and 25,000 wounded. In some units, losses reached ninety per cent of their original number.

General Tadeusz Bor-Komorowski (right), commander of the Warsaw Uprising, is liberated from camp in Austria.
Sikorski Museum

55

September 1939. Units of the 10th Motorized Cavalry Brigade moments before crossing the Polish-Hungarian border to join the Polish Army being formed in France. The army reservists flocked to the garrison towns in Eastern Poland to find their centres of mobilization, then escaped to Rumania, Hungary or Latvia, and through Yugoslavia and Italy to France, where a new Polish army was being formed.

Internment camp in Hungary, Gyujtotabor, November 9, 1939. The picture was taken after a hunger strike that followed the shooting of two Polish soldiers by Hungarian guards. The largest formation in the camp was a battalion of the Polish National Guard "Turka." *Jan Towarnicki*

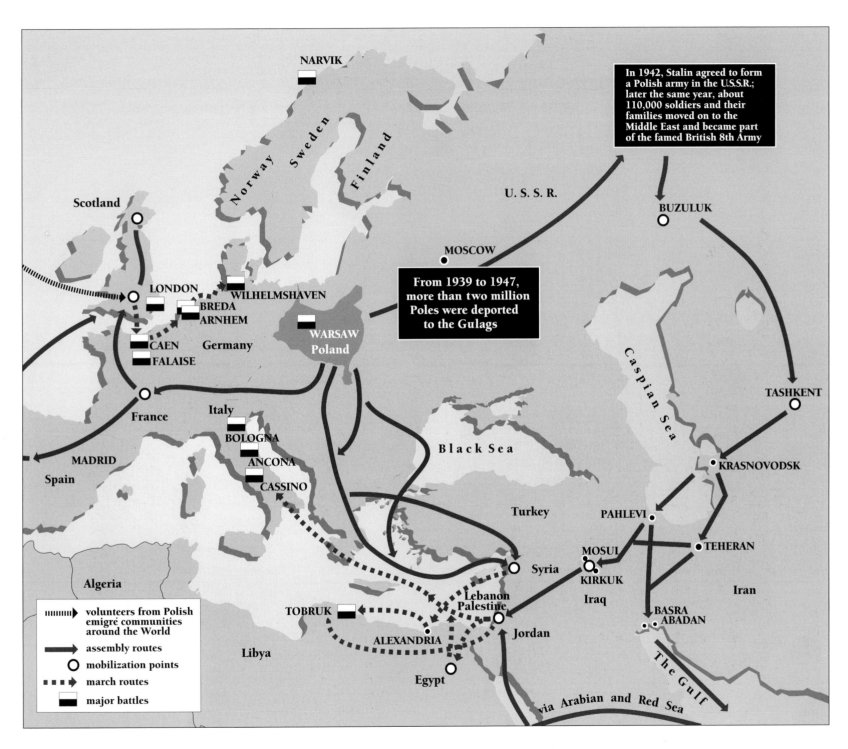

NARVIK

Scotland

U. S. S. R.

BUZULUK

In 1942, Stalin agreed to form
a Polish army in the U.S.S.R.;
later the same year, about
110,000 soldiers and their
families moved on to the
Middle East and became part
of the famed British 8th Army

Norway Sweden Finland

MOSCOW

LONDON

WILHELMSHAVEN

BREDA
ARNHEM

Germany

WARSAW
Poland

From 1939 to 1947,
more than two million
Poles were deported
to the Gulags

CAEN
FALAISE

France

Italy

Caspian Sea

TASHKENT

BOLOGNA

Black Sea

MADRID

ANCONA

KRASNOVODSK

Spain

CASSINO

Turkey

PAHLEVI

Algeria

MOSUL

TEHERAN

KIRKUK

Iran

Lebanon
Palestine

Iraq

TOBRUK

BASRA
ABADAN

ALEXANDRIA

Jordan

Libya

Egypt

The Gulf

volunteers from Polish
emigré communities
around the World

assembly routes

mobilization points

march routes

major battles

via Arabian and Red Sea

Routes the Polish people travelled to continue the fight on all fronts.

Polish cryptanalysts with their French colleagues in front of the building of the Secret Radio-Intelligence centre in Cadix, in Southern France. General Bertrand, the bureau specialist, has said that during their period of operation they broke 673 German signals.
(Far right, Marian Rejewski; centre, General Bertrand)

Special Service and Intelligence

An original V-1 rocket. *Danusia Figiel*

The dedication of Polish intelligence units coupled with several inventions and technical breakthroughs accelerated the Allied victory.

■ From 1933 to 1939, before the Second World War, the German "Enigma" coding system was broken by Polish mathematicians and cryptanalysts Marian Rejewski, Henryk Zygalski, and Jerzy Rozycki. They built doubles of the Enigma coding machine and copies of these were presented by the Polish General Staff to France and Britain at the end of July 1939. In October 1939, a Polish-French decoding centre was launched in France under the code name "Bruno" and this was followed in November 1942 by the Cadix centre. Polish work on Enigma also served as

the basis for British decoding activities at Bletchley. As a result, the Allies were able to read top-secret Nazi orders and cables, which did much to advance their ultimate victory.

■ Engineer Waclaw Struszynski, a Pole on the staff of the Royal Navy, developed a device to locate the position of German U-boats. This turned out to be extremely helpful in charting safe sea routes for Allied convoys.

■ The provision of military intelligence by the Polish Underground was another concrete and effective contribution to the war effort. Any information gathered about German troops and their movements was immediately conveyed to London. Perhaps the single most important

intelligence achievement of the Polish Home Army was the identification of the site where Germany was developing its V-1 and V-2 rockets. The Home Army sent along information about these facilities on the Peenemunde Peninsula, allowing the Royal Air Force to destroy them. When the Germans moved their test sites to Mielec, deep within Poland, the Home Army managed to capture an entire test rocket and arranged to have it air-lifted to Britain.

■ Captain Wladyslaw Wazny parachuted into occupied France and identified the location of 162 flying bomb launchers, later destroyed by the Allied Air Force. He worked behind enemy lines for eleven weeks and dispatched 173 reports before being killed in action in 1944.

Polish engineers at work with mine detectors.
The Polish mine detector was chosen over the British and American inventions as the most sensitive. It detected a shilling at 30 centimetres underground. *IWM - M.H.1138*

Lieutenant J.S. Kozacki was an engineer who designed an ingenious mine detector. Used for the first time in Africa, it doubled the speed at which British troops could move through minefields from 100 to 200 metres an hour. This contributed to the success of British General Bernard Montgomery's 8th Army and was later used by the Allied armies on all fronts. In fact, the same basic design for mine detectors continued to be used by the British Army as late as the 1991 Gulf War.

■ ■ ■

"Two Polish soldiers in Scotland, 'wish we could publish their names,' said the War Office last night — helped to make possible the Eighth Army's advance through Rommel's desert minefields. They produced a gadget with some tin cans, a battery and a few yards of wire.

No one took the two Polish soldiers and their gadget very seriously. 'What is it?' one of them was asked, 'a vacuum cleaner?' The Poles just smiled and went on with their work. One day it was finished, and the gadget was sent to the War Office.

That was nine months ago.

When Montgomery's victorious drive on Tripoli began, the strange-looking gadget, hung together by string and bits of wire, was a working model of the world's first mine-detector. Immediately, it was put into mass production, and two Poles were called for and congratulated by high War Office officials.

And a few days ago the Poles had the best news of all. They heard that their mine-detectors had been largely instrumental in clearing the desert battle area of enemy mines.

Their gadget of a tin can and wire had been a great success. The lives of thousands of British soldiers had been saved.

A War Office official told the *Sunday Pictorial* last night: 'I wish we could publish the names of these two Poles. They have really done a wonderful job'."

Sunday Pictorial on two Polish soldiers who invented a Land mine-detector.
November 22, 1942

A photograph of Home Army soldiers who
drew an unexploded V-1 rocket out of the Bug River.

"They know...how gallantly the Polish Forces have contributed to victory in the field
and in equally dangerous work which produced, among other results, timely evidence
of the German preparations for launching V-1 and V-2 against this country."

The Times on the espionage work of the Polish Underground Army against Germany. November 28, 1944

"That the Germans failed to deliver the holocaust was largely due to the Polish Resistance. Indeed, in a letter to the author, Bomber Command chief, the late Sir Arthur Harris, spells out precisely what would have happened if the Germans had launched the intended number of terror bombs at the very time when the Allies were planning the Normandy invasion and the liberation of Europe....

That, he wrote, would have been the end of the war and the end of England as a free nation. When you see a Pole, doff your hat.

Bring us the proof, London demanded. The Polish Home Army obligated the only way it knew how. It delivered a V-1 flying bomb — one of the terror weapons....

Towards the end of 1943 the V-1 weapon was to be test-fired on Polish soil in the area near Mielec....

One of the great missiles dropped on the sloping banks of the River Bug, close to the village of Sarnaki: and failed to explode. Fully equipped German troops and ragged half-starved Polish patriots rushed to the scene. The Poles won by a short head, rolled the huge device down into the river and disappeared....

For the little group of Polish engineers who battled through the cold nights, surrounded by a thin screen of Home Army tommy-gunners, the task was suicidal. But those dedicated engineers now had but

one purpose in life — to remove the vital parts without explosion. Their own lives matter little....

On that night of July 25, 1943, fate evened the score again and the fragile, unarmed aircraft landed and took off safely carrying a cargo, part of which was 100 lb of scrap metal that had become the most precious treasure on earth. Flying via Brindisi, the aircraft touched down in England the next day....

On the nights of August 17 and 18, 1943, the RAF dispatched a force of 597 bombers which flattened the sinister V-weapon centre."

Christopher Portway, in an article, "When You See a Pole Doff Your Hat," *Saga,* October 1998, London

Mathematicians and cryptanalysts, from left: Henryk Zygalski, Marian Rejewski and Jerzy Rozycki.

■ ■ ■

"The Poles, surrounded as they were by powerful potential enemies, had, between the wars, developed one of the most efficient intelligence services in the world. Their code and cipher bureau, BS4, based in Warsaw and headed by Colonel Givido Langer, had achieved some remarkable successes, including the Battle of Warsaw in 1920, when Polish forces under Pilsudski halted the Bolsheviks at the gates of the city, due in no small measure to the solving of the Russian codes by Polish intelligence.

After this early success, the Poles broke the German Reichswehr ciphers, which they read without difficulty until a certain date in 1928, when a new cipher ('Enigma') began to be used."

Brian Johnson, in *The Secret War*

"As early as 1930, Marian Rejewski, Jerzy Rozycki and Henryk Zygalski, were recruited by the Polish cipher bureau in Warsaw. In the autumn of 1932 Rejewski became aware of the Enigma problem. In a few weeks Rejewski achieved a first breakthrough by establishing a mathematical approach that, in theory, would solve his problem. Then, on 8 December, 1932, he was given what appeared to be authentic documents relating to the German military Enigma. Among them was a list of the keys used in the months of October and December 1931....

Rejewski was now able to put his theory into practice. After only a month of continuous and highly concentrated effort,

he had worked out the electrical connections of the three wheels that were used at that time in the German Enigma. He was able to have a replica of the machine constructed. He began decoding German military messages in early 1933. He was then joined by Rozycki and Zygalski; these three men formed the team that, with the brilliant collaboration of Polish engineers, followed the changes in the German use of the Enigma during the following six years.... They developed a system of *feuilles perforées*, or perforated sheets, due primarily to Zygalski. Zygalski's system of perforated sheets must have been the forerunner of the system developed in the Bletchley Cottage in the fall and winter of 1939/40....

On July, 1939, sensing the approach of war, the Poles decided to make all their

62

achievements known to their counterpartners in France and Great Britain....

On July 25, 1939, to the astonishment of their guest, the Poles explained and demonstrated all their remarkable achievements: their Enigma theory, the models of the German Enigma machines, their 'Cyclometer,' their 'Bomba,' their perforated sheets, and the decodes of German messages that they had produced when the Enigma machine had only three wheels. In August 1939, Polish models of the five-wheel German military Enigma were sent to France and England....

Later, in 1943 to 1945, Rejewski was in England, attached to the Polish army. He was still involved in cryptanalysis, but was not permitted to know how Hut 6 (in Bletchley) had carried on from the start that he had given them."

Gordon Welchman, in *The Hut Six Story, Breaking The Enigma Codes*

■ ■ ■

"Thanks to the Polish-reconstituted Enigma cipher machine and the accumulated data provided by Bertrand's agent Hans Schmidt, the British were thenceforward able to enhance their own cryptanalytical capabilities...

As war approached, Bletchley Park, a converted country estate outside London, had become Britain's cryptological center.

Churchill called the Bletchley people: the geese that laid the golden eggs and never cackled."

John H. Waller, in *The Unseen War In Europe, Espionage And Conspiracy In The Second World War*

■ ■ ■

"Unit 300 continued its work until 8 November 1942, when the Germans occupied the whole of France. Four days later a motorised column entered Uzes and troops smashed down the doors of the Chateau Fouzes; it was empty, though the last member of Unit 300 had barely left through the back door as the Germans arrived at the front....

The Unit dispersed south; some — Rejewski and Zygalski among them (Rozycki had gone down with the *SS Lamoriciere* when she was sunk in the Mediterranean earlier in 1942) — managed to escape over the Pyrenees into Spain, and via Gibraltar, to Britain. Some were caught en route, to be interrogated by the Gestapo. Not one of the captured Poles, though subjected to the most rigorous interrogation by the Gestapo, gave away so much as a hint that Enigma had been penetrated. Many took their secrets to their unmarked graves in German concentration camps."

Brian Johnson, in *The Secret War*

■ ■ ■

"May I in turn congratulate the Sixth Bureau on the careful preparation of the operational parties, and the friendly and efficient co-operation they have accorded to my Officers. Also, I do not forget that what we have been able to achieve this season has been largely made possible by the

people inside Poland, and it is to them that the main credit should be given....

I should be grateful, when the opportunity occurs, if you would convey to the G.O.C. Warsaw my heartiest congratulations."

Letter from The Ministry of Economic Warfare to The Polish General Staff, April 18, 1943

■ ■ ■

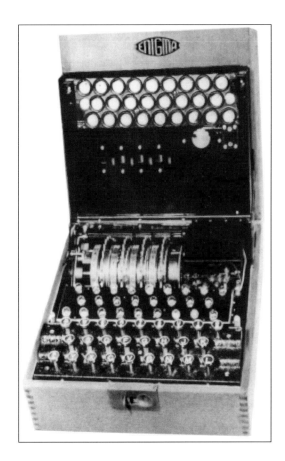

An early model of Enigma, the German coding machine.

Lieutenant-Colonel Roman Czerniawski, code-named "Brutus," was the agent who played a leading role in operation "Fortitude"— the effort to cover up plans for the Allied invasion of the Normandy coast.

Czerniawski remained in France after its collapse in 1940. He organized a network that supplied valuable information to Great Britain. In fact, the chief of British Intelligence stated that his service had never received information that was more valuable than that supplied by "Armand," the pseudonym then used by Czerniawski.

In 1941, Czerniawski and his fifty-four agents were betrayed by his French secretary and captured by the Wehrmacht. The Germans were impressed by the quality and accuracy of his network's records and they decided to persuade "Armand" to work for their side. Czerniawski agreed under one condition: his agents would not be turned over to the Gestapo and were to be treated as prisoners of war.

In the Abwehr, he received his new code-name, "Hubert." An escape was engineered for him in 1942 and he reached England by way of Gibraltar. Upon arrival he immediately reported to General Wladyslaw Sikorski, the Polish Commander-in-Chief and prime minister. He was referred to the British Intelligence Service, which accepted him

Lieutenant-Colonel Roman Czerniawski (born February 6, 1910), the agent code-named "Brutus," was the chief supporting player in operation "Fortitude"— the cover plan of the Allied invasion of the Normandy coast. *Sikorski Museum*

as a double agent, giving him a new code-name, "Brutus."

It was Brutus who informed Berlin that the Allied invasion would take place in Normandy six weeks later than it actually took place. He also said that the "real" invasion would begin in the Pas de Calais. As a result, Hitler redirected his strongest armoured divisions away from Normandy. Once the invasion began it was too late to push the Allied armies back to the sea.

Czerniawski had managed to persuade the Germans to trust him. One of Brutus's

reports, found in the archives of the Ober Kommando, General Jodl, contained a note saying that "material sent by this agent is splendid and very helpful."

After the war, Roman Czerniawski was decorated by both the British and the Poles. He remained in England, serving as a minister in the Polish Government-in-Exile. He died in London on April 26, 1985.

■ ■ ■

"...the part 'Brutus' played in the ground maneuver was potentially the most important. He was to persuade the Germans that the invasion would take place in several installments, the real blow to follow an initial feint.

In May 1944 seven of his reports struck the Germans as so persuasive that they marked the batch as 'uniformly excellent,' with the notation: 'the intelligence supplied by this agent is contributing materially to the clarification of the enemy's order of battle.'

His reports fortified their belief that Normandy would be merely a secondary target, and that a huge American army was being kept in England under General Bradley for the major effort further north. The result is a matter of history."

Ladislas Fargo in *The Game Of The Foxes, The Untold Story Of German Espionage In The United States and Great Britain During World War II*

64

Jan Kozielski

Code-named "Karski." Courier of the Home Army. Took information about Polish underground activities to Britain and the Allies. Went to London in 1942 with a special report about the situation and prosecution of Jews in the Warsaw Ghetto.

Elzbieta Zawacka

Code-named "Zo." Courier of the Home Army. The only woman trained in England by the Polish Paratroop Brigade. Parachuted into Poland in 1943. Decorated by the British and the Poles with Virtuti Military and in 1996 with an Order White Eagle — the highest Polish decoration.

Antoni Kocjan

In charge of a special section of the intelligence service of the Home Army. Located the base of the manufacturing plant of V-1 and V-2 rockets on the Usedom Island and sent the report to England. The plant was bombed by Britain on September 17, 1943.

Kazimierz Leski

Code-named "Bradl." Outstanding officer of the intelligence service. Travelled through Europe as Wehrmacht General von Hallman.

Zofia Rap-Kochanska

Code-named "Marie Springer." Organized a Polish intelligence network in Germany.

Tadeusz Garlinski

Code-named "Odrowaz." Officer of the Home Army. In charge of action "Submarine" in the Phillips factory. Used a special substance that caused corrosion of radios in German submarines. Damage developed only when the ships were well at sea.

Parthenay, February 1940. The Supreme Commander, General Wladyslaw Sikorski (left), meets a French general during the oath-taking ceremony by the Polish 2nd Infantry Division.

France 1939 - 1940

During the First World War, Polish soldiers from Poland and from many emigré communities around the world — including Canada — had come to France to join the Polish army corps forming there. This happened again in 1939. Polish soldiers came by many different routes. Some skied across the Carpathians. Some arrived by way of prisons in Hungary. A few stole boats and rowed down the Drava River into Yugoslavia. Many had come by steamer to Marseilles. Altogether, more than 70,000 soldiers and volunteers made their way to France to fight the Germans.

The pale blue uniforms Polish soldiers received from France dated from the First World War.

The creation of a Polish Army on French soil was initiated soon after the outbreak of the war, at a time when the defence of Poland reached its peak. On September 7, 1939, a special Polish-French military agreement was signed to provide for the establishment of a regular Polish Army on French soil to fight alongside the armies of France. This unit was placed under the command of General Wladyslaw Sikorski, a hero of the 1920 war against the Soviets.

France itself was mobilizing five million men and thus was experiencing a shortage of arms and equipment. The large numbers of Polish soldiers escaping from Eastern Europe were not able to bring their own arms. As a result, there was a serious problem in providing the Polish units with the necessary weapons, uniforms and shelter. American and British equipment arrived at a very slow pace. Many experienced men and their units were forced to wait for equipment right up to the moment when the Germans began their attack. In fact, English uniforms destined for the Polish Army arrived in May of 1940, just as France collapsed, and had to be sent back without being unloaded.

Within ten months of the German attack on Poland, General Sikorski had put together an army of 85,000 men on French soil. It was composed of the 1st Grenadier Division, the 2nd Riflemen Division, the Light Mechanized Brigade, the Independent Podhale Riflemen Brigade, units of two infantry divisions and seven airborne wings.

The Polish airmen who came in large numbers through Rumania and Hungary were later incorporated into the RAF, and units of the Polish fleet were placed under the command of the British Navy.

The Polish Army fought with distinction during the Battle of France. Two Polish infantry divisions, one armoured unit, and twelve anti-tank companies took part in the defence of France. The Grenadier Division fought in the Saar, on the Marna-Rhein Canal and in the defence at Lagarde. The Riflemen Division fought in Champagne and after numerous clashes with the enemy crossed over to Switzerland. The Polish Navy participated in the Battle of the Atlantic, while the Polish Air Force took part in the defence of Paris.

Clockwise from top left: Polish soldiers arrive at Coetquidan, France, after the defeat of Poland in 1939; volunteers and recruits on the way to the Coetquidan training camp; Polish Morane fighters at Lyon-Bron airfield, March, 1940. *Marian Fijal;* Polish airmen at the Lyon-Bron airfield.

German armoured units cross the French border.
For Germans, the sections of the front line defended by Poles often were the only difficult points to cross. German prisoners of war commented that wherever they met with strong resistance, they were positive Poles were on the other side.

Polish

Polish soldiers fought for France with no less ardour than they fought for Poland. They remained faithful to the Franco-Polish alliance even as France fell before the German onslaught.

The fall of France was a tremendous disappointment to the Poles. Yet, they did not give up their struggle against Hitler. They decided to continue the war from Britain, the only European country that was still free and capable of waging a war against the Nazis. The challenge, however, was to evacuate an army of nearly 85,000 men, who were scattered in different parts of the country and some of whom had not yet completed their basic training.

On June 17, 1940, General Wladyslaw Sikorski sent an appeal to British Prime Minister Winston Churchill with a request for the evacuation to Britain of the Polish units in France. The next day he flew to London to see Churchill personally. From two in the afternoon, for two hours, he met the British General Ismay and officials of the British Admiralty, describing the exact locations of various units of the Polish Army in France as well as the ports toward which they were fighting their way to escape from France.

The first orders to the British Navy were issued at three o'clock, shortly after Sikorski's meetings started. At seven o'clock, the first Polish troops were taken off. Evacuation from the ports of St. Jean-de-Luz and Bordeaux was completed seven days later without a single casualty. The Poles who streamed in from all parts of France arrived in a state of complete exhaustion. France was unprepared for the war, and there was insufficient food, clothing and shelter available for the armed forces. In many places, French civilians actually asked the retreating armies to pay them for food and sleeping quarters.

A handful of Polish soldiers escaped from Brittany to England in fishing boats. As the French campaign drew to a close, they bought civilian clothes, a few bottles of wine, water and cheese, and then they walked for several miles to a small fishing village. They boarded a fishing boat and set sail for England at night. After two days they reached the port of Falmouth, where they were greeted with warm hospitality and received food, cigarettes and clean clothes, and then were taken to Portsmouth.

One of Poland's destroyers, *Blyskawica*, participated in the evacuation of
Allied forces at Dunkirk. *Sikorski Museum.*

"'Blyskawica' went south and established a new line along the swept channel which had
been cleared towards the Dunkirk shallows. All through the day she helped the growing
number of ships in the flotilla carrying out the evacuation. That night, with two of her British
flotilla mates, she received orders to go into Dunkirk.
At midnight, and in a heavy bombing attack, they reached the entrance to the harbour. One
plane of the attack detached itself from its formation and came down to less than 1,000 feet,
spraying 'Blyskawica's' decks with machine-gun bullets. The Poles opened fire in
reply and the plane crashed shortly afterwards.
Still under desultory attack, she put her boats in the water to pick up men from the beaches in
obedience to instructions, but at 1:45 a.m. these orders were cancelled and she was
sent back to work on patrol, this time in the vicinity of the North Goodwin light vessel...."

A.D. Divine in *Dunkirk*

On June 20, 1940, most of the Polish 2nd Division, 14,000 men in full gear, crossed the Franco-Swiss border as if on parade. They were welcomed by an astonished and delighted local Swiss population. Showing no signs of being discouraged, their first question was how best to reach Britain or Palestine.

Top: The Polish 2nd Division crosses the Swiss border — singing the Polish anthem.

Left: Soldiers of the Polish 2nd Division enter the internment camp in Switzerland.

"The Prime Minister said that he had that morning seen General Sikorski, who had just returned from France. The General had told him of his experiences during his 8-10 days on the French Front. The French troops had seemed paralysed in the face of the German onslaught, and had disappeared into houses before the advance of the German tanks. The German troops were not particularly formidable, but the French morale seemed to be low. On the other hand, the Polish troops had fought very well and had been highly complimented by General Weygand, who had said that with a few more Polish divisions he could have stemmed the tide. Polish troops were now marching on Bordeaux, and wished to be evacuated in order to continue fighting. If any way possible, arrangements must be made to embark them. Polish pilots had been instructed to fly any machines they could get hold of to England, and they seemed to be experiencing no difficulty in flying off with French aircraft. There was a Brigade of Poles at Brest, but he was afraid that it was too late to take them away.

The Secretary of State for War said that arrangements had been put in hand at Bordeaux and Marseilles to take off any Czech troops who wish to leave, but he would much prefer to embark Polish troops."

War Cabinet minutes — June 19, 1940, cabinet papers, 65/7. Crown copyright material in the Public Record Office, London, is reproduced by permission of the Controller of Her Majesty's Stationery Office, PRO - CAB 65/7

Discussing plans in the field on the road near Borkenes. Left to right: Lieutenant Kwiatowski, Major Ilinski, liaison officer to British GHQ; Brigadier General Zygmunt Szyszko-Bohusz, general OS Polish Forces, and Captain Starkiewicz, chief of the Fourth Bureau. *IWM - N.144*

Norway

On April 9, 1940, the Germans attacked Norway. To stem the assault, the Allies sent troops to Narvik. Operating in France, the Polish Independent Podhalanska Rifle Brigade was sent into battle. Under General Zygmunt Szyszko-Bohusz, it played an important role in the storming of Narvik.

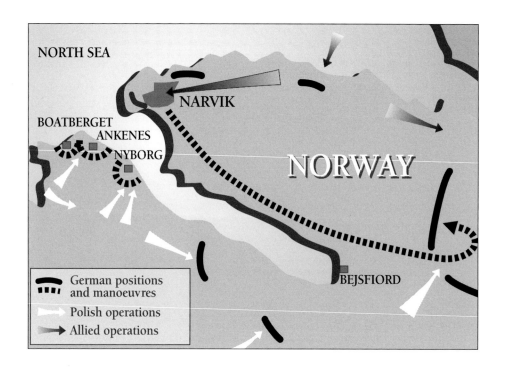

The Polish unit was ordered to embark at Brest on April 22-23, 1940, and it reached the Norwegian port of Harstad on May 7. It then took part in the storming and occupation of Bjervik, and in a brilliant attack supported by British and French artillery, it occupied the towns of Ankenes, Nyborv and Bejsfiord. Because of a deteriorating situation in France, however, the Brigade received an unexpected order to withdraw on the night of May 30. To ensure the safety of the troops, all their heavy equipment was left behind and destroyed. The Polish troops were even ordered to throw their hand-grenades overboard. They reached the port of Brest on June 14 but three days later news arrived that the French soldiers were in full retreat. Shortly thereafter, the campaign ended with the surrender of France.

The Polish Independent Podhale Riflemen Brigade before leaving for Norway.

Soldiers of the Independent Riflemen Brigade on board the Allied ship *Chenonceau* en route to Norway. They left from Brest Harbour on April 23, 1940, and after two weeks, on May 7, reached the port of Harstad.

Members of the Polish Armed Motorcycle Patrol in action at Borkenes with Bren guns. *IWM - N.147.*

A fishing smack leaves a Norwegian harbour with supplies for the Polish Army at Narvik.
On the wheelhouse, a Bren gunner stands guard. *IWM - N.184*

A Polish soldier back in Harstad from the Narvik front sleeps on a quay. *IWM - N.301*

Polish and Canadian troops enter Caen.

FRANCE

POLAND

France 1944 - 1945

When the battle of France ended, the Polish Armed Forces on French soil did not surrender. Instead, they crossed into Switzerland, travelled to Palestine or found their way to Great Britain. After four long years, they returned to France on the heels of the Normandy invasion as part of the British and Canadian forces.

"A Polish Armoured Division is fighting with the Allied armies in France. It went into action first on
August 8th as part of the Canadian First Army, attacking in the direction of Falaise....
The Poles are burning to reach Paris, not because it is Paris, but because it is just that much
nearer to Germany."

Correspondent of *The Times* on the Polish Armoured Division in France (under Major-General Stanislaw Maczek). August 11, 1944

Tanks of a reconnaissance regiment near Caen.

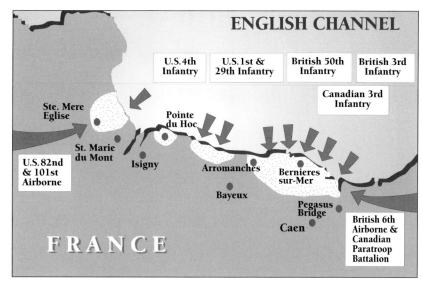

ENGLISH CHANNEL

U.S. 4th
Infantry

U.S. 1st &
29th Infantry

British 50th
Infantry

British 3rd
Infantry

Canadian 3rd
Infantry

Ste. Mere
Eglise

Pointe
du Hoc

St. Marie
du Mont

Isigny

U.S. 82nd
& 101st
Airborne

Arromanches

Bernieres
sur-Mer

Bayeux

Pegasus
Bridge

Caen

British 6th
Airborne &
Canadian
Paratroop
Battalion

FRANCE

Actual advance

On June 6, 1944, Allied forces landed on the Normandy beaches of France.

The Battle of Normandy lasted for three months. By August 1944, the Canadian 1st Army had driven a wedge into the German line, heading south to join up with the American 3rd Army. The Germans, fearing encirclement, redoubled their defence.

The Polish 1st Armoured Division, under the command of General Stanislaw Maczek, landed on the beaches of Normandy on August 4, 1944. On August 8, the division was incorporated into the Canadian 2nd Corps and was given the task of breaking the German line at Falaise and closing the route of the enemy withdrawal. Before the battle, General Maczek said:

"We are bringing into the battle something which the Germans now lack. We are bringing our enormous moral strength. We are bringing the full awareness of the fact that we are fighting for a just cause."

The Poles attacked with their Canadian comrades on August 12. A fierce battle continued for a week without pause.

At the end, the Poles were cut off from their Allies, without the possibility of supply or evacuation of the wounded. Even so, they single-handedly blocked the advance of two battle-hardened German SS corps. The carnage in front of the Poles was perhaps the bloodiest of the battle. The last German reserves of tanks and heavy equipment were destroyed here.

Once the battle of the Falaise Gap was over, German resistance in France began to crumble.

Polish soldiers disembark in Normandy in the area of Arromanches-Les Bains.

On July 30, 1944, the first units of the 1st Armoured Division land in France in the area northwest of Caen. On August 8, they started operating as part of the Canadian 2nd Corps of the Canadian 1st Army.

A rare moment of rest for an Anti-Tank Platoon before the attack on Potigny on August 15, 1944

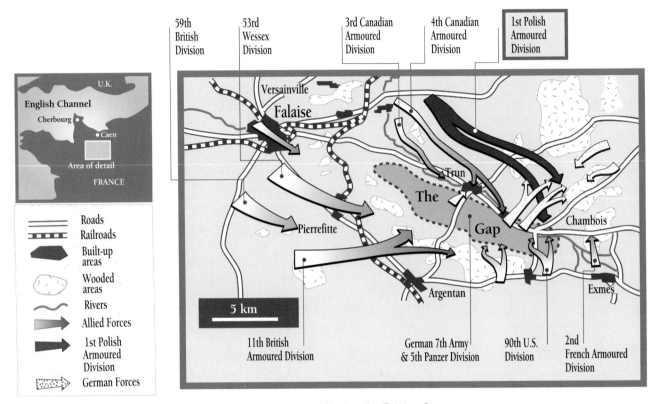

59th
British
Division

53rd
Wessex
Division

3rd Canadian
Armoured
Division

4th Canadian
Armoured
Division

1th Polish
Armoured
Division

U.K.

English Channel
Cherbourg
• Caen
Area of detail
FRANCE

Versainville
Falaise

Trun

The

Gap

Chambois

Pierrefitte

Argentan

Exmes

Roads
Railroads
Built-up
areas
Wooded
areas
Rivers
Allied Forces
1th Polish
Armoured
Division
German Forces

5 km

11th British
Armoured Division

German 7th Army
& 5th Panzer Division

90th U.S.
Division

2nd
French Armoured
Division

Closing the Falaise Gap.

"It was the Poles who took the brunt of the attempted German break-out. The enemy had concentrated in all probability the
last remnants of the tank forces which had been operating in and around the pocket.
This entire force, with supporting infantry, bore down on the Poles, who were temporarily out of touch with their Allies on either flank.
The Poles stood their ground. Compelled to face about — for the enemy force had approached them from their rear — and with
both their flanks exposed, they fought back all day against the Germans, who emerged in wave after wave from the cover
provided by the forest of Gouffern....
Though small parties of Germans succeeded in getting through the Polish lines,
the great bulk still remained within the trap when night fell...."

Correspondent of *The Daily Telegraph*, H.D. Ziman, on the role of the Polish Armoured Division in the Battle Falaise-Chambois on August 21, 1944

After the Falaise-Chambois Battle. Soldiers of the Canadian 4th Armoured Division passing the Falaise battleground said:
"Bloody Poles, what a job!" They ordered a sign posted: "A Polish Battlefield."

"It was the Poles — actually an Armoured Division — under the Command of General Maczek, who, as it is only now officially disclosed, played a leading role in sealing the Allied victory in Normandy, closing on 21st August the gap which was the only remaining outlet for the battered German army east of Argentan. During six days of very heavy fighting the Polish Division took upon itself all the fury of two German SS Corps, taking about 5,000 prisoners, including one General and 140 officers."

British Ministry of Information's account on the role of the Polish 1st Armoured Division in the Falaise-Chambois Battle from August 15 to 21, 1944. August 28, 1944

General Stanislaw Maczek, commander of the 1st Armoured Division, is congratulated by his officers
on the victorious battle at Falaise-Chambois.

"The battle of Chambois was an engagement of decisive significance. Your Division was
like the cork of a bottle in which the Germans were trapped...."

Speech by Field Marshal Sir Bernard Montgomery, Commander-in-Chief of the British Army of the Rhine, during his visit
to the Polish 1st Armoured Division in Germany. November 25, 1945

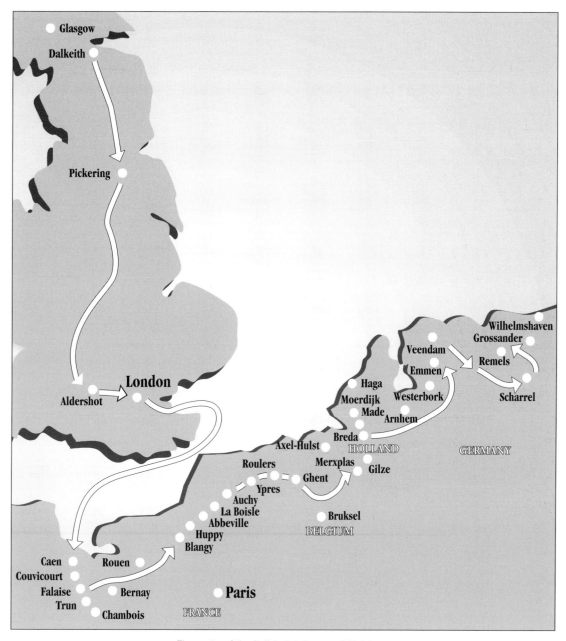

The route of the Polish 1st Armoured Division.

The Polish 1st Armoured Division landed in France from Great Britain on August 1, 1944, and on August 8 fought the famous battle of Caen. On August 17, it was they who succeeded in closing the Falaise Gap. They fought at Ypres from September 6 to 8, and entered Breda on October 14. They were the very first to march into Ghent. Their commander was the great General Stanislaw Maczek, who fought in Poland in 1939 and who commanded the Polish Armoured Brigade in the first battle of France. General Maczek died on December 11, 1994, in Scotland, at the age of 102.

After General Mittelhauser ordered the discontinuation of hostilities in Syria, Polish troops crossed from that country to Palestine with their equipment to join forces with the British. In the photograph, members of the Carpathian Brigade unload kit and equipment on arrival at their camp site in Palestine. *IWM - E.330*

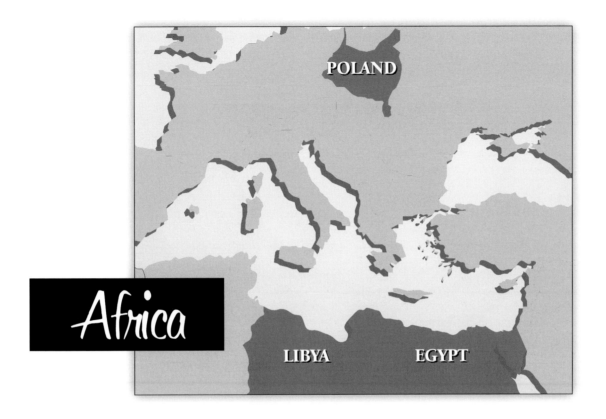

Africa

As France fell in the summer of 1940, and the Polish forces there withdrew to Britain, another Polish unit continued the fight in the Middle East. The Carpathian Brigade, a unit formed in French-held Syria, denounced the French surrender and crossed the border into Palestine, where it put itself at the disposal of the British authorities. As a result, this brigade became the first unit of the Polish Army to join battle under British command.

Palestine, July 1940. After the French armistice, Polish troops from Syria disregarded the orders to surrender and crossed to Palestine, joining forces with the British. Living in tents, they underwent a period of rigorous training. *IWM - E.334*

Palestine — Latrun, October 1, 1940. Closing camp before moving to Egypt.

Poles arriving in Syria began to coalesce into a fighting force as early as January and February of 1940. At that time, the units formed part of the French Army in the Middle East. Called the Polish Independent Carpathian Brigade, the unit was under the command of General Stanislaw Kopanski. By the time France fell, the unit numbered 3,000 fighting men.

Following the terms of the French surrender to the Germans, the French commanding officer, General Huntziger, ordered the Polish units to lay down their arms. General Stanislaw Kopanski refused, preferring instead to leave Syria with all of his military equipment intact. The situation became extremely tense and Kopanski was even threatened with arrest. Thanks to secret assistance from another French general, de Larminat, the Poles marched out of Syria with all of their equipment and joined the British Army in Palestine.

The brigade was later transferred to Egypt, where it became part of the British 8th Army. British warships transported the Brigade to Libya, where it fought until early 1942.

In Libya, the brigade took over the defence of the difficult western section of the city of Tobruk, and later the city's long eastern section. In this action, it fought alongside Czechoslovak and Australian battalions. The Poles formed a deep friendship with their comrades, especially the Australians. The standing joke became that during the next peace conference they would demand a joint frontier between Poland and Australia.

The brigade distinguished itself in the battle of Gazala. During this engagement, the Polish soldiers participated in the main attack on the enemy, advancing over completely unprotected rocky terrain.

The brigade continued to grow in numbers and by the end of the Libyan campaign numbered nearly 6,000. After victory in Africa, the Carpathian Brigade was transferred to Palestine, where it joined forces with Polish troops from Russia. As a result, it was transformed into the 3rd Carpathian Rifle Division.

Polish troops leave an Egyptian port for Tobruk. Soldiers wait to board a Man-o'-War that took them to the garrison. *IWM - E.5055*

A general view of the quayside shows Polish troops boarding ship for Tobruk. *IWM - E.5056*

Twenty-five-pound guns fire on enemy positions outside Tobruk. *IWM - E.6561*

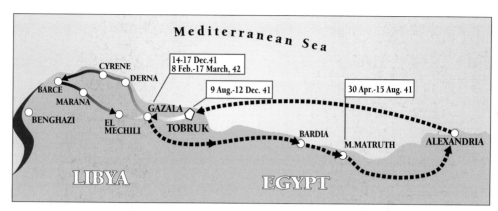

Routes of the Independent Carpathian Brigade.

"I have been spending time today in Tobruk's front line with men who have come here because they have chosen to fight for an idea which is more important than life and stronger than death. They are part of the Polish forces which are helping the Australian-English garrison to hold Tobruk, and the idea they are fighting for is the liberation of their country — and Europe — from Nazi domination.

Today I have talked with officers and men who have neither homes nor homeland. Many of these men do not know whether their families are alive or dead because they have not heard of them since Poland fell.

They have been in Tobruk's front line only a few weeks, but already tales of their daring are being told.

A handful of men from the regiment I visited today stormed an enemy strong post a few nights ago. It was a stone-walled miniature fort defended by machine-guns and mortars, but the Poles closed in under hot fire and annihilated 20 Italians inside. One Italian was captured. He tried to give his captors the slip in the darkness and regain his own lines. He was shot dead."

Correspondent of *The Manchester Guardian* on the Carpathian Brigade in Tobruk. October 24, 1941

"Since they came to Tobruk, Polish troops under the cover of night, have raided the Italian lines three times. Their last attack just over a week ago was the most daring and successful.

An Italian machine-gun post on a hilltop overlooking the Polish lines was their objective. For weeks it had spat death across a deep gully of no-man's land among the Poles crouching behind a few rocks.

Laden with hand grenades and with their bayonets at the ready, the Poles made a nightmare journey across the exposed country, lit now and then by the flash of heavy gunfire. Overhead, enemy bombers droned on their way to Tobruk harbour.

The Poles descended 300 feet into the wadi, climbed its almost perpendicular other side into the enemy's lines and crawled round the machine-gun post to attack from the rear. When the alarm rang out, the startled Italians pumped machine gun bullets into the night and bigger guns opened up. The Poles charged, hurling grenades as they ran.

Outnumbering the Poles by two to one, the Italians fought fiercely but soon gave way before their terror of the bayonets. Twenty Italians lay dead and over 50 had been wounded when the Poles withdrew. One Pole was killed and three wounded."

Correspondent of *The Daily Telegraph* on the fighting of the Carpathian Brigade in Tobruk. October 24, 1941

97

November 14, 1941. General Wladyslaw Sikorski, the Polish premier and Commander-in-Chief, visits Tobruk and inspects Polish troops.
He arrived on board a British torpedo boat, stopping on the way to Moscow for talks with Josef Stalin. *IWM - E.6559*

Polish soldiers of the Carpathian Brigade man artillery in position at Tobruk, September 1941. Until these positions were taken over by the Poles, the longest period of defence had been four weeks. On December 10, 1941, the brigade raised a white-and-red flag at the top of Medauar Hill.

"During the night of 1 January, 1942, two units of the First and Second South African Divisions attacked at the point of the bayonet strongly defended localities held by the enemy covering the town of Bardia.

The units actually engaged in this dashing attack were the South African, Kaffarian Rifles and the Royal Durban Light Infantry, closely supported by British tanks and medium artillery, by the Polish Field Artillery Regiment and by the New Zealand Cavalry Regiment.

Rather than face a repetition of this bold, skillfully organised attack, the enemy decided to surrender unconditionally. The whole operation was magnificently supported by H.M. ships, which heavily bombarded enemy concentrations and artillery positions in the forward area and also engaged with equal effect many objectives on the rear of the enemy defences."

Communiqué issued by British GHQ, Cairo, on the Bardia Battle. January 4, 1942

■ ■ ■

"I watched the Poles make their great attack last night. This was the battle for Gazala and the road to Bomba, and there were British, Indians and New Zealanders in it as well. To the Poles went the honour of leading the attack from the centre north-westwards towards the coast.

They had sallied out from Tobruk, carrying everything before them. They had manned old war-strained trucks and guns which they inherited from the Australian garrison. They added to these captured German staff cars, troop-carriers, and they were provisioned on captured German bread, meat and pickles. Some captured vehicles had Kookaburras painted on them, some Swastikas and some Polish emblems. They had seven different varieties of machine guns.

And now, under General Kopanski, a slight little man with one bad eye and a fantastic record, they were asked to lead all the Allies up the coast. After they had been cooped up in Tobruk for three months, this was their first chance to advance and strike in the open."

Alan Moorehead, war correspondent, in *The Daily Express* on the Polish Carpathian Brigade at Gazala. December 17, 1941

99

10, Downing Street
Whitehall.

On behalf of the Government and people
of Great Britain, I am very glad to write
this line of welcome to every Polish soldier,
sailor or airman who has found his way over
to help us fight and win the war.

I have heard of the difficulties which
have beset your journeys to this country: I
realise the hardships which your relatives
and friends are undergoing in Poland: but I
know that these will only inspire you to
further deeds of endurance and valour for
which your nation is so justly renowned.

Until the hour comes when through our
united efforts you return to your own country,
we in Great Britain hope that you will find
amongst us a happy, if temporary, home.
Together with our joint Allies, we look forward
to the day when victory will crown our efforts
and we shall help to build a new and better
Europe. I know that the Polish forces on
land and sea and in the air will play a worthy
part in achieving this goal.

Winston S. Churchill

3rd September, 1940.

Prime Minister Winston Churchill welcomes the Polish
Armed Forces in a letter written on September 3, 1940

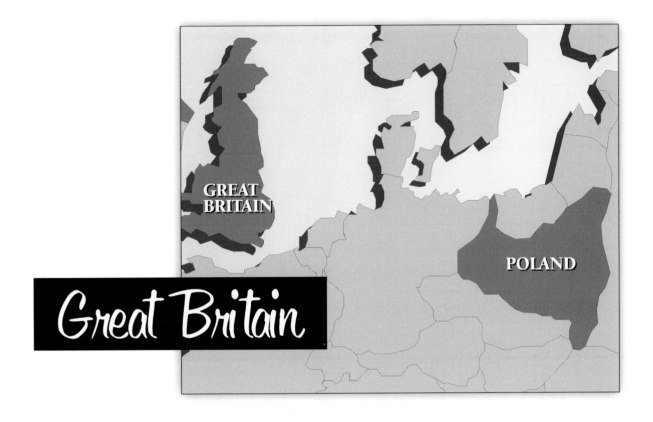

Great Britain

In June of 1940, as France succumbed to the German onslaught, representatives of the Polish Armed Forces contacted the British government. On June 18, 1940, General Wladyslaw Sikorski met with British Prime Minister Winston Churchill and quickly came to an agreement on the evacuation of the Polish Armed Forces from France to the British Isles. The Royal Navy dispatched a task force to the Bay of Biscay to accomplish this, opening a new chapter in the annals of the Polish Forces.

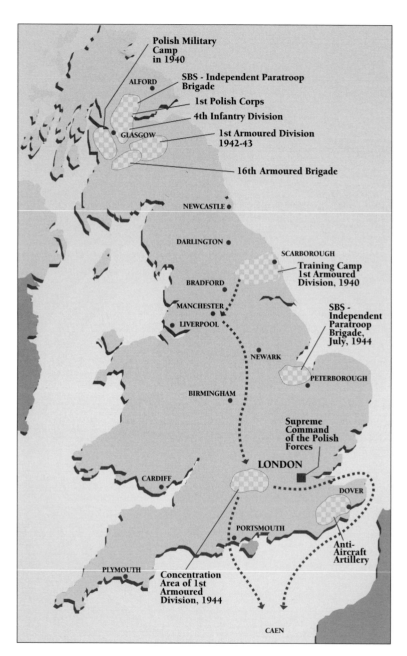

Location of Polish Armed Forces training camps.

The map includes the following labels:

Polish Military Camp in 1940
SBS - Independent Paratroop Brigade
1st Polish Corps
4th Infantry Division
1st Armoured Division 1942-43
16th Armoured Brigade
ALFORD
GLASGOW
NEWCASTLE
DARLINGTON
SCARBOROUGH
Training Camp 1st Armoured Division, 1940
BRADFORD
MANCHESTER
LIVERPOOL
SBS - Independent Paratroop Brigade, July, 1944
NEWARK
PETERBOROUGH
BIRMINGHAM
Supreme Command of the Polish Forces
LONDON
DOVER
CARDIFF
Anti-Aircraft Artillery
PORTSMOUTH
PLYMOUTH
Concentration Area of 1st Armoured Division, 1944
CAEN

Polish airmen receive awards from General Wladyslaw Sikorski. Northolt, 1941

Training camp in Crawford. *Sikorski Museum*

The first units of the Polish Armed Forces to arrive in Britain after the outbreak of the Second World War were ships and submarines of the Polish Navy that were able to escape from the Nazi-controlled Baltic Sea. Polish bomber crews followed shortly afterward.

In 1940, army units arrived from France. During the critical autumn and winter of 1940-41, they joined British troops along stretches of Britain's shores, guarding them from an invasion that was expected at any moment. The Polish Forces in Great Britain were reorganized into the 1st Army Corps, which included the 1st Armoured Division and 4th Grenadiers Division, as well as other units.

They were to distinguish themselves during the Normandy invasion and the final assault on Germany. In August 1944, the 1st Armoured Division participated in the battle of the Falaise Gap. It then fought numerous other engagements as it accompanied Field Marshal Montgomery's 21st Army Group through France, Belgium, Holland and Germany. The Independent Polish Paratroop Brigade fought at Arnhem.

The Polish Air Force in Britain consisted of fourteen squadrons and was larger than the combined air forces of all other exiled nations. It played a major part in all operations of the RAF, most notably during the Battle of Britain in the summer and autumn of 1940, when Polish fighters accounted for fifteen per cent of all enemy planes shot down.

Incorporated into the Royal Navy, the Polish Navy participated in numerous naval actions, in the Channel, the North Sea, the Atlantic and the Mediterranean. It fought at Narvik, Dunkirk, Lofoten, and Dieppe. And it participated in the convoys that sailed to Murmansk, to Malta convoys, and to the beaches of Normandy.

Soldiers of the 1st Corps build defence constructions along the coastal line where an enemy landing was expected. *Sikorski Museum*

Summer, 1940. Polish Armed Forces train in Scotland. *Sikorski Museum*

Training centre in Scotland. Future parachutists are shown the correct way to land. A Polish paratrooper is taught how to keep his parachute from dragging him along the ground after he lands. *IWM - H17879*

Training centre in Leven.
An airborne brigade blows up a shelter during a practice on September 24, 1942. *Sikorski Museum*

Scotland, 1942. Prime Minister Winston Churchill with General Wladyslaw Sikorski and General Charles De Gaulle, chief of the Free French Forces, at a Polish tank demonstration.

"I was very glad to see the Polish Forces in Scotland. Their smart and resolute bearing convinced me that when the call for action comes, they will confirm the reputation for soldiery and audacious bravery which they and their comrades have already won on the battlefields of Poland, France and Norway.

Poland has shed her blood in the same cause of Right and Freedom for which we in England are fighting, and now in the hour of her misfortune we watch with admiration the indomitable will of her sons, wherever they may be, to fight on till the enemy has been defeated. Though their country be trampled underfoot by the oppressor, the Polish people, who have struggled so long and so honorably for their natural existence and independence, will in the end achieve their heart's desire."

Prime Minister Winston Churchill's letter to General Wladyslaw Sikorski, Comander-in-Chief Polish forces and Polish prime minister, after his visit to Polish troops in Scotland, October 27, 1940

■ ■ ■

"Ever since Mr. Winston Churchill paid a visit 'to the Polish front,' all the world has known that the army of Poland is in Scotland and is playing an operative part in its defense. It holds an important sector, and the ardour, intelligence, and skill that all ranks put into their military duties bode ill for the invader who should attempt to secure a footing in its neighbourhood.

Between the Polish forces and those whom they would immediately defend, a most friendly relationship has been established.

Joint exercises are carried out with the Home Guard, with whom the closest cooperation has been established, in spite of the difficulties of language."

The Times' special correspondent on Allied Forces in Britain, May 13, 1941

A member of the Polish Airborne trains in 1942. *IWM - M.H.1229*

On duty at camp. *Sikorski Museum*

Polish soldiers perform extra "duties" during their stay in Scotland. *Sikorski Museum*

Polish soldiers were very warmly welcomed on British soil. After arranging all formalities, they were sent to Glasgow to special military camps. At first they were quartered in tents and temporary barracks. Because they were unused to the cold Scottish autumn and winter, the Poles soon experienced outbreaks of pneumonia and rheumatic fever. The situation improved, however, when they were moved to better quarters.

Friendships flourished between the Poles and the Scots, and the homes of many Scottish families were opened wide for the Polish soldiers. The overwhelming kindness of their hosts made the Polish solders feel at home. Soon they were singing Scottish songs while the Scots learned Polish tunes.

Many collaborative Polish-Scottish ventures arose. For example, exhibitions of Polish art were held under the auspices of the British Council as a result of the efforts of Professor Harvey Wood. With the help of Sir John Ervine, principal of the University of St. Andrews, professors Wright, Snodgrass and Baxter set up special facilities to accommodate Polish students studying for final exams or to teach English to Polish tutors. This historic university also conferred honorary degrees on General Wladyslaw Sikorski and the Polish president in exile, Wladyslaw Raczkiewicz. Initiated by Professor Baxter, the Polish-Scottish Society organized lectures and concerts. Special free courses in the Polish language were organized in Glasgow, Edinburgh, Kincardine, and Perth. Newlywed Scottish wives of Polish soldiers organized a Women's Auxiliary Service to help the Polish Army.

Polish soldiers spend their time off with Scottish girls. *Sikorski Museum*

Aircraft of the Polish Army Co-operation Squadron on a photographic reconnaissance over snow-covered Scottish mountains. *IWM - H.1770*

"Napoleon complained that the British soldier was too stupid to know when he was beaten.
The Germans have found that Polish airmen suffer from a similar defect. They refuse to acknowledge defeat.
They trekked out of Poland and fought in France.
They found their way to Britain...."

Speech of the Secretary of State for Air, Sir Archibald Sinclair, in opening the London exhibition of Polish Air Force in Great Britain, March 9, 1944

Polish Air Force

King George VI and General Wladyslaw Sikorski inspect Polish airmen.

Despite only a very brief interval of independence after 1918, Poland was able to assemble a significant air force. In fact, before the Second World War, Polish aviation had a number of achievements to its credit, including Stefan Drzewiecki's work in aerodynamics, Czeslaw Tanski's construction of prototype gliders and helicopters, Orlinski's 1926 journey by air from Warsaw to Tokyo and back, Ludwik Idzikowksi's attempted crossing of the Atlantic from east to west in 1928, and Stanislaw Skarzynski's 1933 crossing of the Atlantic in a light sporting craft. Three Poles — Franciszek Zwirko, Jerzy Bajan and Zdzislaw Plonczynski —

distinguished themselves in sporting aviation by winning international touring competitions. And Poland's LOT Airlines flew a regular route between Salonica and Europe, one of the longest in Europe at the time.

As a result, Poland had no shortage of well-trained pilots when war broke out. What it lacked, however, was a sufficient number of modern aircraft. Mass production of newly designed aircraft had only started and too few were available when Poland was attacked on September 1, 1939.

The first German attack on Poland involved 2,700 aircraft, a number that rose to 3,350 within five days. With only 400 aircraft at their disposal, Polish

airmen accounted for some 800 downed German aircraft. To excuse these disproportionate losses, the German air marshal, Hermann Goering, misled the media into thinking that the Polish Air Force actually had 800 planes. When the Soviet Union attacked Poland from the east on September 17, 1939, the Polish Air Force flew whatever planes it could to Rumania and Hungary, where the pilots were interned and the equipment confiscated. Their escape from Rumania was described by René Curtis in *Winged Tenacity*:

"I was with the Ambassador at the Polish Embassy one day when a Rumanian Jew was announced. He

111

wished to see the Ambassador on a matter of special importance. He was admitted and revealed his plan for the escape of 2,000 Polish airmen. All he wanted in return was £5 per head for every airman delivered safely at Marseilles. The Ambassador was surprised and rather skeptical. How could such a number get away under the German nose, so to speak. And it was explained that the main snag was the presence in Bucharest of a number of escapees at once, if noticed by the German authorities. There was a way round that. He (the Rumanian) knew the Home Secretary very well and would arrange with him that the city should have a black-out exercise on the night the airmen would be passing through. All they would have to do was to go to the railway station. They would speak to no one. They would board a train which they would find in a special siding. The train, naturally, would be blacked out and no questions would be asked.

The Ambassador agreed to the plan. He paid £1 per head as the airmen left Rumania and the remaining £4 for each man were to be paid, on arrival at Marseilles, by the Polish authorities in France. And so the plan went through. The airmen took the train as arranged, reached Constanza unseen and shipped away before the Germans could stop them.

Other airmen dwindled away in ones, twos and threes by bribing the camp guards.

Another day, at the Embassy, a Rumanian military policeman arrived and asked to see the Polish Air Force authorities. He had with him one Polish pilot. This man, he said, was the sole remaining internee in his camp and the authorities had discovered the racket which had been going on. He therefore wished to hand him over to Poles and claim the price which had been put on every Polish airman's head."

The escaping Polish airmen re-emerged on the battlefields of France and joined the French Air Force. They were dispersed among various French squadrons and took part in the defence of France, taking down sixty-nine enemy planes while losing only fifteen pilots. In a number of cases, it was the Poles who were the last to leave and the last to protect essential war industries: they defended the Bloch aircraft factories at Chateauroux and they covered the evacuation of French Air Force personnel from Rochefort. After the capitulation of France, most of these Polish airmen were transferred to Britain. Again, René Curtis describes an escape from France:

"Many French pilots who wished to get out of France and continue the struggle found difficulties in their way. The French authorities had categorically forbidden any French pilot to leave French soil. So they appealed to their Polish colleagues to lend them Polish uniforms in which to board ships bound for England. There was one funny scene

when there were not enough Polish uniforms to go round. The French pilots stood on the quay, amidships, and, as the Poles got aboard, they took off their uniforms and threw them down to the waiting French, who promptly put them on and queued up for the gangway."

According to the Polish-British military agreement of August 1940, a separate Polish Air Force was formed as part of the RAF. With fourteen squadrons, it was stronger than the combined air forces of all the other nations in exile. Polish fighter pilots took part in intruder patrols, the air offensive over France and Belgium, screening the Dieppe raid, the defence of Malta, the attack in Tunis, D-Day, and all the campaigns of 1944-1945. They also helped to defend London against flying bombs. Polish bomber squadrons were assigned to most of the more important raids on Germany military targets, both in Germany and in the countries occupied by Germany. And the Polish squadron attached to Coastal Command participated in the Battle of the Atlantic.

The Poles played a decisive role in the Battle of Britain. The number of "kills" by Polish fighters was so high that it can be said their contribution turned the tide of this campaign, one of the most important of the war.

Polish airmen also distinguished themselves in night raids and aerial photography. Some pilots were sent to Africa, where they flew thousands of long-distance sorties across Africa to the Middle East.

"Somewhere in England, as announced by the Secretary of State for Air in the House of Commons on Tuesday, the first detachment of the Polish Air Force is already training with enthusiasm to form itself into the first of several squadrons that will soon become part and parcel of the R.A.F.

Despite the ordeal they have undergone, the spirit of these airmen is as strong as ever. R.A.F. officers, who have had the task of getting their Polish 'recruits' housed in an R.A.F. Station, are full of admiration for their new charges. One officer of great experience said: 'Those who have arrived so far are a magnificent body of men. All have plenty of actual flying experience and they are full of enthusiasm, yet show a quiet determination to get on with their job as quickly as possible....'

When the history of the war comes to be written, the Polish squadrons of the R.A.F. will claim their part. That is the overwhelming obsession of these young men."

Air Ministry's announcement on the first detachment of the Polish Air Force in Great Britain, December 13, 1939

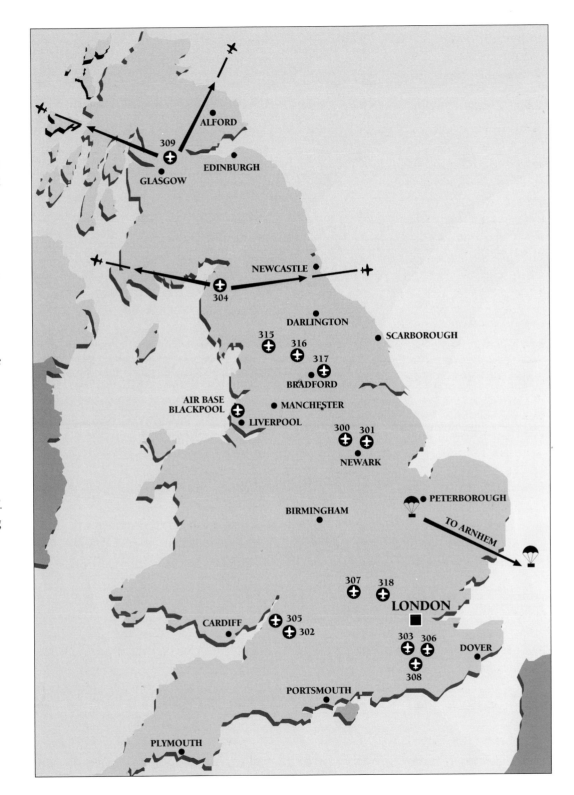

Location of Polish fighter squadrons.

Members of 303 Squadron. From left: Jan Daszewski, Zbigniew Kustrzynski, Wojciech Kolaczkowski, Wladyslaw Urbanowicz, Tadeusz Arentowicz, Jerzy Radomski

"Another pilot praised the courage of the Poles. 'They are tremendous fighters,' he said. 'Their enthusiasm is infectious. When they go tearing into the enemy bombers and fighters they go so close you would think they were going to collide'."

Air Ministry News Service, September 8, 1940

■ ■ ■

"Wherever the British and Allied pilots went, the Poles were sure to follow. Moreover, they stayed on the job to the last, and they never once shirked their duties. In fact, it has become a general practice that whenever a difficult and very dangerous task was to be executed the Polish airmen were usually called upon to perform it. As for their losses, it is no exaggeration to say they were very heavy and commensurate with the great risks they took and the reckless courage with which they fought. This dash and recklessness inherited from these valiant ancestors produced the type of a perfect airman."

Stefan Kleczkowski in *Poland's First 100,000 — Story Of The Rebirth Of The Polish Army, Navy And Air Force After The September Campaign, Together With A Biographical Note About Its Creator, General W. Sikorski*

Battle of Britain

Polish airmen played a vital part in the Battle of Britain. At the peak of the fighting, every eighth pilot was a Pole. This enabled the exhausted Fighter Command to maintain its operational strength by replacing killed and wounded British pilots. The quality of the Polish pilots counted even more than their numbers. No. 303 became the highest-scoring fighter squadron in the RAF.

Polish pilots of 303 Squadron.

"It is not often, however, that we realise that there are over 10,000 men in the Polish Air Force in this country. There is one squadron, however, No. 303, whose exploits have long been the admiration of all Poles and Allied forces. They have destroyed more German planes than any other individual squadron.... They are typical Poles. Courage and cheerfulness are their predominant characteristics, together with a passionate love of their country and an undying hatred of their enemy."

Article in *The Daily Sketch* by Lieutenant-Colonel Cazalet, MP, September 1, 1942

Captain Eugeniusz Horbaczewski of 315 Fighter Squadron paints a symbol marking the fourth V2 he shot down over England on his aircraft. *IWM - M.H.1937*

"Polish fighter pilots were well represented in the ranks of the famous 'few' of the Battle of Britain. There were two entirely Polish squadrons: the 302, City of Poznan, Squadron and the 303 Kosciuszko Squadron. Moreover, a large number of the Polish fighters fought individually in many different R.A.F. squadrons.

During the Battle of Britain, Polish fighter pilots accounted for a large number of enemy aircraft destroyed and damaged.

On September 15th, 1940 Air-Marshal Sir Trafford Leigh-Mallory, as he then was, sent the Polish fighter squadron the following message: — 'The Germans have made a great effort today and you have played a notable part in frustrating it. Heartiest congratulations to you all on your splendid results'.

The Battle of Britain's days are as vivid in the memory of the Poles at home and abroad as they are to the people of Britain."

Air Ministry News Service on the Polish Air Force in the Battle of Britain, September 16, 1944

Top: A bomb is inscribed: "In return for Warsaw."
Sikorski Museum

Bottom: Pilots inspect remnants of the 178th German aircraft downed by 303 Fighter Squadron.

126 "Hitlers" downed during the Battle of Britain, recorded in cartoon fashion on one of the Hurricane aircraft of 303 Squadron.

Captain Aleksander Onoszko, 304 Bomber Squadron.
Stanislawa Onoszko

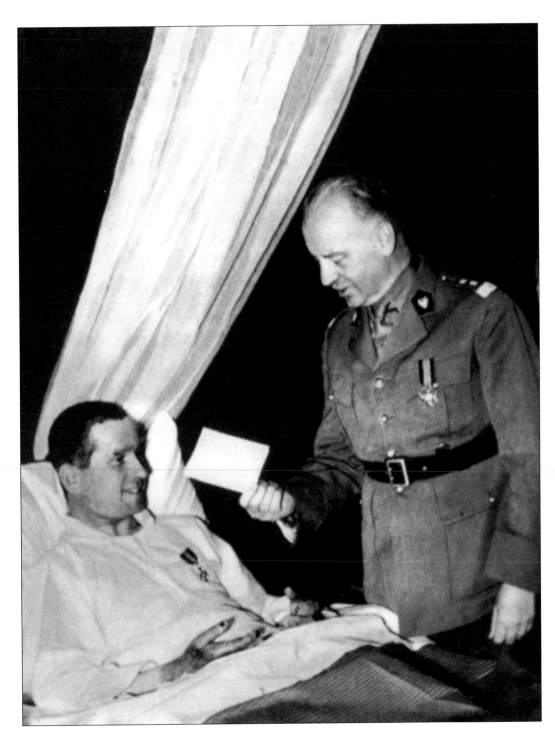

General Wladyslaw Sikorski decorates Major Zdzislaw
Krasnodebski, first commander of 303 Squadron, injured
during an air battle on September 6, 1940

Crew of No. 304 Bomber Squadron, Wing B, in front of a Wellington NZ-T. *Stanislawa Onoszko*

"For their part the bomber squadron have carried out 3,200 raids and dropped 9,000 tons of bombs on enemy targets. No fewer than 120 airmen have been decorated. The figures eloquently epitomise an inspiring enterprize. The rise of the Polish Air Force from the tragic ruins and seeming obliteration of September 1939 symbolises the undying spirit of the whole nation. Its own motto 'We shall return' expresses both a faith and a resolve. The strength of the Polish Air Force is now double what it was at the outbreak of the war with Germany. Its losses have not been light. All told, 1,000 of its members are listed as killed, missing or captured. Many rest in the cemetery at Newark. The stone cross under whose shadow their graves lie is inscribed: 'For Freedom'."

The Times in an article on the shooting down of the 500th German aircraft by the Polish Air Force in Great Britain, January 1, 1943

Polish airmen scramble at the Polish airfield station in Northolt.

Areas bombed by the Polish Air Force

Paratroop landings and supply drops

Major fighter battles

Major air bases

Operations of the Polish Air Force during the Second World War.

Victory Parade. London, May 1945

This empty frame is a symbol of the absence of Polish Armed Forces in the Victory Parade in London in 1945.
The political arena, and Joseph Stalin's rule in the new communist Poland, effectively prevented the Allies from acknowledging the strong part played by Polish Armed Forces in the major battles of the Second World War. However, as a token of recognition for their great performance during the Battle of Britain, members of the Polish Air Force were the only Polish fighters invited. But General Mateusz Izycki, commander of the Polish Air Force, as an act of solidarity with the Polish Armed Forces, answered:
"With regret, but we can not accept this offer."

"During the Battle of Britain, Polish pilots accounted for 273 enemy aircraft. They were a small part of the not very large force which faced the Luftwaffe in those days; but it may give you some idea of their achievements when I tell you that they alone brought down fifteen per cent of the total Luftwaffe casualties.

When Mr. Churchill spoke his famous words — 'never in the field of human conflict was so much owed by so many to so few' — he spoke of the Polish fighters as much as of our own pilots."

Speech of Air Officer Commander-in-Chief, British Air Force of Occupation, Germany, Air Chief Marshal Sir Sholto Douglas, at the opening of the RAF Exhibition in Warsaw, November 15, 1945

Stanislaw Skalski, top gun, in his Mustang aircraft. During the Second World War he scored 21 planes downed, two probably downed and one damaged.

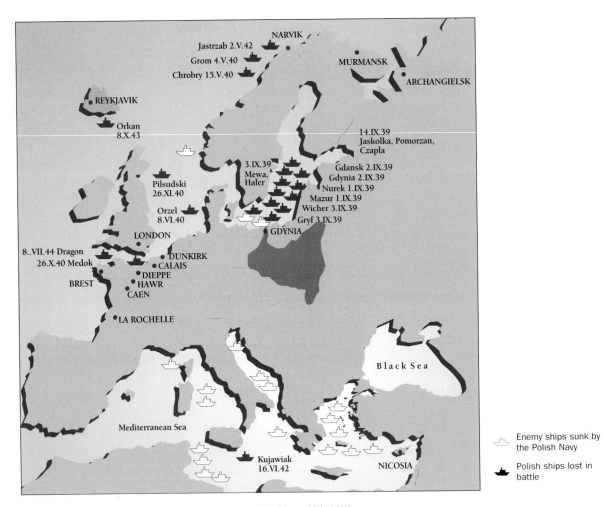

Polish Navy operations in the Second World War.

Polish Navy

The Polish submarine *ORP Dzik* rests after battle. In the background is *ORP Burza*.

When Poland regained its freedom in 1918, it had only limited access to the Baltic Sea. As a result, it was late in developing a navy. At the beginning of 1939, Poland had a small number of destroyers, submarines, auxiliary ships and merchant vessels but it was at a significant numerical disadvantage in relation to the German Navy. Despite its small size and the overwhelming nature of the German assault, the Polish Navy did play a memorable part in the defence of Gdynia, the Hel Peninsula and Westerplatte. Polish ships and coastal batteries brought down fifty-three German aircraft, sank two German destroyers and damaged the battleship *Schleswig-Holstein*.

As Polish resistance weakened under the German assault, three Polish destroyers, *Blyskawica, Grom* and *Burza,* and two submarines escaped from the Baltic Sea and arrived in Britain. They were incorporated into the British Navy and took part in a number of subsequent engagements. Later, their numbers were increased by the addition of several new units built in British shipyards.

The Polish Navy participated in the attack on Narvik by shelling shore batteries and engaging German raiders. They covered the evacuation of the British Expeditionary Force from France by shelling the coast around Dunkirk. *Blyskawica* even entered the Dunkirk canal, where it experienced heavy bombing and machine-gun fire. From 1940, the Polish destroyers took part in the Battle of the Atlantic. They escorted convoys and patrolled the North Atlantic continuously. They also took part in operations at Tobruk and Dieppe and in an attack on the German-occupied Lofoten Islands. Other activities involved protecting shipping in the English Channel, patrols and escorting convoys in the Mediterranean, as well as engagements at Oran, Sicily and Italy.

The Polish submarine *ORP Orzel* arrives in a British port. The submarine, operating in the Baltic, was forced to enter the neutral port of Tallin in Estonia to save the life of a sick commander. It was interned and stripped of all important navigational equipment. It escaped from illegal internment on September 17/18, 1939, without maps, charts, or gun locks. Forty-two days after its famous escape, it arrived at a British port. On June 11, 1941, a short communique was issued by the Polish Naval headquarters in London: "The return of the submarine *Orzel* being overdue, it must be presumed lost."

"When Poland was wantonly attacked by Germany, she had a small but highly efficient modern navy. Three Polish destroyers and two submarines joined up with the British Navy. The story of the escape of the submarines from the Baltic has been described by a British writer as 'one of the greatest epic adventures in the whole story of submarining.' It will assuredly take its rightful place in the proud annals of the Polish Navy....

In view of its small size, the number of operations in which the Polish Navy has taken part is almost incredible, especially bearing in mind that some of them are continuous. Amongst these operations are Narvik, Dunkirk, Lofoten....

The Poles are justifiably proud of the part played by their Navy in the sinking of the 'Bismarck.' A Polish destroyer was the first ship to sight the 'Bismarck.' (May 26th, 1941). The British Captain of the Destroyers Flotilla (which included the Polish destroyer) signaled congratulations to the Polish Commander for dauntlessly attacking the 'Bismarck' in spite of the great disparity of the two ships in size and armament."

Speech of First Lord of the Admiralty A.V. Alexander when he opened a London exhibition on the Polish Navy. February 10, 1944

A Polish destroyer readies for action in the Atlantic.

Cleaning cannons before action. *Sikorski Museum*

Loading food supplies on *ORP Garland*. *Sikorski Museum*

"The other day, in a well-known British harbour, I inspected the crew of a Polish destroyer. I have rarely seen a finer body of men. I was stirred by their discipline and bearing.

Yet how tragic was their plight: their ship was afloat, but their country had foundered. But, as I looked around upon all the great ships of war which lay at their anchors, and at all the preparations which were being made on every side to carry this war forward at all costs as long as may be necessary, I comforted myself with the thought that when these Polish sailors have finished their work with the British Navy, we will take particular care that they once more have a home to go to...."

Speech over BBC by First Lord of the Admiralty Winston Churchill. March 30, 1940

Preparing torpedoes.

A torpedo starts its course.

129

"Just below periscope depth the *Sokol* was caught in a torpedo net. Enemy motor-boats appeared and one arrived over the submarine before she got free, after eight minutes. Her commanding officer said it was 'not a nice situation,' but he went back the next day and, avoiding the net, torpedoed an enemy destroyer. Two nights later he torpedoed a fully laden merchant ship bound for Africa."

Captain G.W. Simpson, commander of British submarines operating from Malta, on the flotilla's achievements in the last two years, quoted in *The Manchester Guardian*. April 3, 1943

ORP Sokol leaves the Mediterranean in 1944. The captured Nazi banner and the Jolly Roger are trophies of their battle victories, showing enemy ships sunk by torpedoes or fire. The cross-hatches on the flag commemorate the only action in the war when the ship entered an enemy port — by penetrating through enemy submarines and nets — and safety escaped.

Gun drill on board *ORP Piorun*. The destroyer, formerly *HMS Nerissa*, was handed over to the Polish Navy by the British Government to replace *ORP Grom*, the Polish destroyer that was bombed and sunk off Norway. *IWM - A.2497*

"The Nelson touch was introduced with good results in a recent action when a Polish light coastal craft, on early morning reconnaissance, intercepted six German E-boats. The Polish craft went straight for the enemy force which, taken by surprise, was driven off.

Before the action the order came: 'Return to base.' The message, however, was not understood by the lieutenant commanding the vessel. The commanding officer of the base said: 'I am not without suspicion that this misunderstanding was a case of turning the blind eye, and if so results fully justified this following of precedent'."

The Sunday Times on the action of a Polish coastal craft. August 2, 1942

"For such a small navy, these losses are very severe, but they have only served to intensify the Polish fighting spirit. Survivors immediately asked how soon could they be given another ship in which to continue the fight; they are all determined again to get the enemy as quickly as possible...."

Gordon Holman in *The Little Ships*

Top: The bodies of a few of the many killed on *ORP Dragon* during the invasion of France.

Bottom: British pilots shot down by the Germans are rescued by *ORP Slazak*. The *Slazak* had "luck" in finding shot-down Allied pilots. In the British Navy and Air Force, she had the nickname *Shepherd*.

Just before its single-handed attack on the *Bismarck*, *ORP Piorun* approaches a Royal Navy tanker. *ORP Piorun* is in the foreground.

A French commander arrives on board as the Polish destroyer *ORP Piorun* co-operates with the French forces. *Sikorski Museum*

"Details are now available of the very gallant and efficient part played by the Polish destroyer *Piorun* (Commander E. Plawski) during the destroyer phase of the operations against the *Bismarck*.... It was from the Piorun that the first sighting of the *Bismarck* was made shortly after 10:30 on the night of 26th May.... The *Piorun* herself engaged the *Bismarck* with her armament in the most spirited manner...."

An Admiralty communique. June 8, 1941

A quiet moment during lunch time. *Sikorski Museum*

Christmas at sea — letters from their families.

"Throughout the days of the disasters, from Norway and Calais to the Moles of Dunkirk, the Polish Navy had carried its share of the burdens; it had borne its share of the loss — and the loss to the Allies in that period had been very heavy. Of the First Flotilla with which they had worked so long, 'Burza' and 'Blyskawica' were almost the last survivors. Ten ships out of the 13 of the original force were gone....

The Polish Navy was down: It was by no means out. The story of its regeneration after Dunkirk is as magnificent as the story of the days which preceded it....

It is not possible to measure fame or to make assessment of self sacrifice, but in the four years since the Polish Navy fired the first shot in this greatest of all wars her people have won from the British Navy 11 D.S.Os., 22 D.S.Cs and 29 D.S.Ms. The British Navy does not give awards lightly. If measure be wanted, it is here....

And yet to-day the Polish Navy is stronger than ever it has been in its history. After more than four years of war it has a record of fighting, a career of service, that challenges comparison with the navies of the world."

A.D. Divine in *Navies In Exile*

On board the Polish destroyer *ORP Piorun*. When they get a chance, which is not very often, sailors sling their hammocks and make the most of it. Their usual bed at sea is the deck. *IWM - A.2487*

General Wladyslaw Sikorski signs the Polish-Soviet declaration in Moscow, December 4, 1941, as, right to left, Soviet Marshal Josef Stalin, Soviet Foreign Minister Victor Molotov, Ambasador Stanislaw Kot and General Wladyslaw Anders look on.

Russia

On July 22, 1941, Germany attacked its former ally, the Soviet Union. On July 30, the Polish
Government-in-Exile in London signed a Polish-Soviet Agreement that provided for the release of
all Poles deported into the Soviet Union and the formation of a Polish Army in the U.S.S.R.
The army created as a result of this agreement eventually went to the Middle East. Thousand of Poles
were left behind in the U.S.S.R., however, because they could not get permission to leave.
They were later formed into another unit that fought under Soviet command.

First recruits.

On September 17, 1939, Soviet troops entered Poland from the east in support of the German attack that had come from the west. This had been provided for in the Ribbentrop-Molotov agreement, according to which nearly half of Poland was to be handed over to the Soviet Union. Over the next two years, more than two million Poles, regardless of sex or age, were forced from their homes and deported into the vast interior of Russia.

Once the Nazis turned against their Soviet allies, the Polish government in London resumed diplomatic relations with the U.S.S.R. It also entered into an agreement that provided for the organization of a Polish army on Soviet soil. According to this agreement, Polish soldiers and civilians taken into Soviet concentration camps and prisons after the Soviet invasion of Poland were to be released and allowed to join a newly forming Polish army.

A steady stream of Poles found their way to the recruiting centres set up in Russia by General Wladyslaw Anders, himself a former Soviet prisoner. Volunteers travelled thousands of miles under very harsh conditions to sign up. They came from distant Lake Baikal, the borders of Manchukuo (Japanese-occupied Manchuria) and the farthest reaches of Siberia. As a result, however, Polish officers and entire Polish families were saved from death at the hands of their Soviet captors.

The first parade of the new army took place in early September 1941. As General Anders reviewed these hungry recruits, dressed in rags, without shoes and without equipment, he could not have predicted that this would eventually become the Polish 2nd Corps, perhaps the single most famous Polish fighting unit of the Second World War.

The recruiting centres were located on the Volga steppes, between

138

Polish generals Wladyslaw Anders (left) and Wladyslaw Sikorski are greeted by Russian military officials. They were full of hope for the future of a Polish Army being organized on Russian soil.

Kuibyshev and Chkalov. Three infantry divisions were formed in Buzuluk on the Volga River, in Tatishchev, Totskoye and in Koltubyanka. Initially, these units endured extremely difficult conditions. In fact, during this initial period, they were focused more on survival than on training. Quartered in tents as temperatures dropped to lows of –50° C, they did not even look like an army: the first British uniforms did not arrive until November.

On December 4, 1941, an addendum to the Polish-Soviet Agreement allowed General Anders to increase the strength of the Polish Army to six divisions totalling 96,000 men. Of these, he would be responsible for equipping two divisions and feeding 44,000 people. The rest of army was to depend on support from the Western Allies. The agreement also provided for relocation of the recruiting and training centres to Uzbekistan. From January 13 to 25, 1942, Polish units organizing in the Soviet Union were transferred to southern Asia.

New volunteers continued to arrive at the recruiting centres but many were in a desperate condition. It was estimated that about two per cent of those arriving died within a few days and ten to twenty per cent were ill. Their exhausted condition weakened their resistance and led to frequent epidemics.

Tensions

grew between the Soviet Union and the emerging Polish army. The Soviet authorities went back on their initial agreement and began making every possible difficulty about releasing their Polish prisoners. They also attempted to weaken the Polish forces by reducing their food allowance from 44,000 to 26,000 portions. It took a personal intervention by General Anders to reverse this decision and restore rations to the original level.

Relations became explosive when questions were raised about the disappearance of 15,000 Polish officers and soldiers who had been imprisoned by the Soviets after September 1939. Despite numerous interventions by General Anders, by General Wladyslaw Sikorski, and by the Polish ambassador, it proved impossible to establish even a trace of their whereabouts. The matter was even raised directly with Soviet Premier Josef Stalin, all to no avail.

Polish mistrust of the Soviet Union reached back two decades to the Polish-Soviet war of 1920. The Soviet invasion of Poland in September 1939 did nothing to reduce that mistrust. Now the Soviet authorities were impeding efforts to create a Polish army on Soviet soil and they absolutely refused to say anything about the disappearance of the 15,000 Polish officers. Given these deteriorating relations, General Anders took the decision to move the Polish Army out of Russia. In March 1942, it began its evacuation to British-controlled Iran and the last Polish Army transport crossed the Iranian border on August 25, 1942. Altogether, 114,000 Polish soldiers and civilians left the Soviet Union, leaving behind:

415,800 registered Polish graves
434,300 lost and dispersed persons
681,400 persons to whom the Soviet authorities did not give permits to leave.

Despite promises to keep them open, Polish recruitment centres in Russia were immediately liquidated by the Soviet authorities. The Soviets had been obstructionist and unco-operative but they chose to accuse Anders of betrayal. In an act of petty vengeance, on January 16, 1943, they reversed an earlier decree reinstating citizenship rights to the Poles still held in Russia. They justified this on the grounds that the Polish people had betrayed their Soviet ally because Anders had led his army out of the Soviet Union.

Recruits receive their first Russian "uniforms" — coats and hats. The first British uniforms arrived in December.

Top right: Future commander of the 2nd Armoured Warsaw's Division, Bronislaw Rakowski (as Colonel Rakowski in photograph, on page 215.)

Top left: Volunteers wait for hours to be accepted into the army.

Bottom right: A cemetery in Buzuluk, winter, 1941. In Polish recruiting centres alone, from March until May 3,800 soldiers died. How many died on the way to the centres nobody knows.

Below: Polish children arrive at a recruiting centre. They often travelled on their own.

Polish soldiers train with wooden cannons and guns, the first "arms" received from Russia.

Buzuluk, November 1941: A special mass celebrates Polish Independence Day (November 11). Sitting in front is General Wladyslaw Anders.
At this time, the first uniforms were just being issued.

Soldiers of the 5th Infantry Division take part in field exercises in Tatishchev.

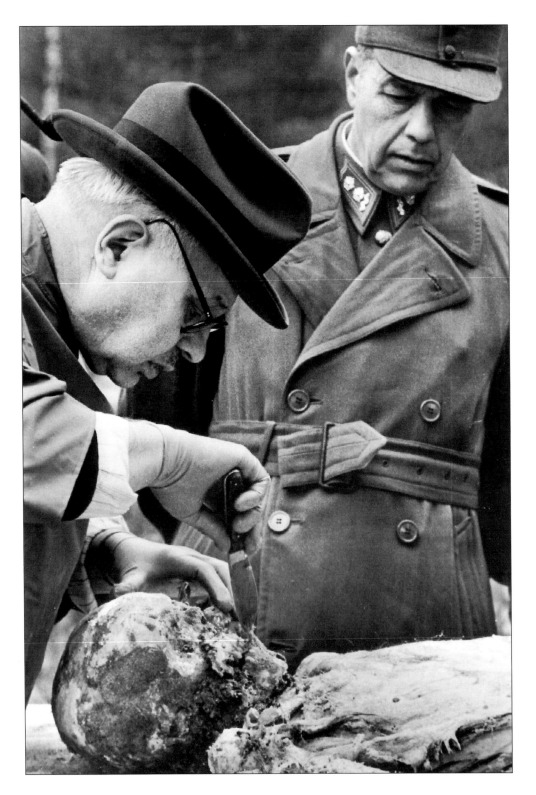

Dr. F. Orsos, the Hungarian delegate, examines the skull of Victim 835 of the massacre of Katyn, identified as Roman Zwierzchowski. Orsos stated that the massacre had taken place at least three years earlier.
Germany and Poland had requested that the International Red Cross investigate the Katyn graves, but the Soviets prevented this. The Germans, instead, organized an international medical commission and invited distinguished professors and specialists in forensic medicine from twelve European countries. *IWM - H.U.82777*

Katyn

Location of the prison camps at Kozielsk, Starobielsk, and Ostashkov where Polish officers and men were killed.

At the beginning of 1943, German units participating in the invasion of the Soviet Union uncovered a mass grave near the village of Katyn. Further investigation quickly showed that this was the final resting place of more than 4,500 Polish officers imprisoned by the Soviets in September of 1939 and murdered by the NKVD the following year.

The officers found at Katyn were only part of a much larger group of 15,000 military and professional men who disappeared after they were taken prisoner by the Soviets. At the outbreak of the war, they had been deported from Poland as part of a systematic Soviet campaign to eliminate any leaders who might oppose them. They were sent to three prison camps — at Kozielsk, Starobielsk and Ostashkov. In the spring of 1940, they were killed and buried in mass graves.

In 1943, the Germans overran this part of the Soviet Union. They found traces of mass graves and exhumed the bodies. Given the atrocities being committed by the Nazis in occupied Europe, it was supremely ironic that the German army reported their discovery to the Swiss Red Cross, accusing the Soviets of mass murder.

Confronted with grisly and public evidence of their crimes, the Soviets categorically denied that they had caused the murders. Typically, they turned the tables and blamed them on the Germans. Furthermore, they forced the Allies to silence Poles who were outraged by this crime. No one was ever punished for these murders and for fifty years the Soviets continued to deny them. It was not until 1993, following the collapse of the Soviet Union, that the Russian government finally and officially admitted the Katyn massacre.

СССР
**НАРОДНЫЙ КОМИССАРИАТ
ВНУТРЕННИХ ДЕЛ**

марта 1940 г.
№ 794/Б

г. МОСКВА

ЦК ВКП(б)

товарищу СТАЛИНУ

В лагерях для военнопленных НКВД СССР и в тюрьмах западных областей Украины и Белоруссии в настоящее время содержится большое количество бывших офицеров польской армии, бывших работников польской полиции и разведывательных органов, членов польских националистических к-р партий, участников вскрытых к-р повстанческих организаций, перебежчиков и др. Все они являются заклятыми врагами советской власти, преисполненными ненависти к советскому строю.

Военнопленные офицеры и полицейские, находясь в лагерях, пытаются продолжать к-р работу, ведут антисоветскую агитацию. Каждый из них только и ждет освобождения, чтобы иметь возможность активно включиться в борьбу против советской власти.

Органами НКВД в западных областях Украины и Белоруссии вскрыт ряд к-р повстанческих организаций. Во всех этих к-р организациях активную руководящую роль играли бывшие офицеры бывшей польской армии, бывшие полицейские и жандармы.

Среди задержанных перебежчиков и нарушителей гос-

т. Калинин - За
т. Каганович - За

С подлинным верно
Главный государственный архив
Российской Федерации   Р.Г.Пихоя

9.

A copy of a document dated March 5, 1940, ordering the shooting of Polish officers from three camps — Kozielsk, Ostashkov and Starobielsk. Signed across the printed text by Josef Stalin, Klimient Woroszylow, Vyacheslav M. Molotov and Anastas Mikojan.

"4,421 people were murdered in the Katyn forest, 3,820 in Starobielsk near Kharkov, 6,311 in Ostashkov district. 7,305 were killed in other POW camps and prisons in the Ukraine and Byelorussia, the burial places still being unknown.

Among professional army men imprisoned in camps there were 13 generals and numerous graduates of the Higher Military School. 8,411 officers and reserve officers made up the cadre which would be able to cover at least 16 divisions. Among the reserve officers there were at least 730 university professors, primary and secondary school teachers, at least 920 medical doctors and veterinary doctors, more than 420 lawyers, 630 engineers and 45 priests of different religions, parliamentary deputies, civil servants, diplomats, land owners, famous sportsmen including Olympians.

The crime of genocide was ruthlessly and purposely committed in order to weaken the Polish nation and destroy its top intellectuals."

Stefan S. Baluk in *Poles On The Frontlines Of World War II 1939-1945*

An international delegation inspects the grave site. Large numbers of victims were neatly stacked face down. They were arranged in this position after they were killed, or they had been forced to lie down on top of their dead comrades before they were shot.

IWM - H.U.74966

149

"They were almost all educated professional men — doctors, civil servants, teachers — and each one had his hands tied behind his back, and a German bullet in the base of his skull."

Norman Davies in *Heart Of Europe — A Short History Of Poland*

150

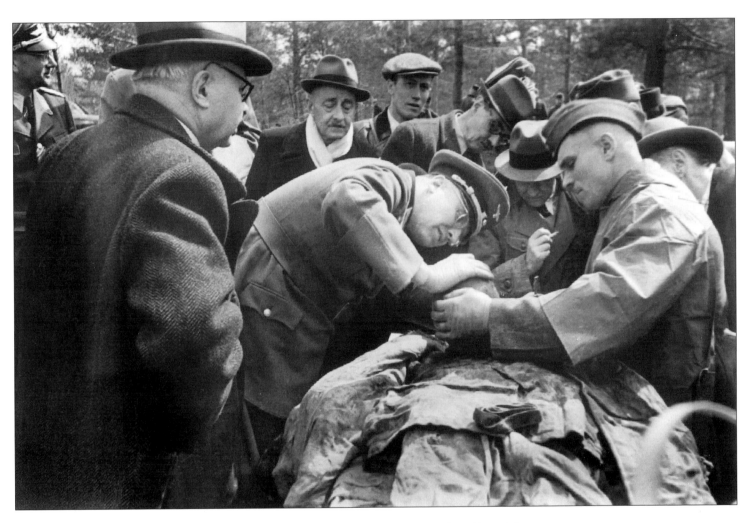

Forensic medicine specialists of the international delegation examine a Katyn victim. *IWM - H.U.74965*

Under Soviet Command

On duty at Sielce camp.

After the evacuation of General Wladyslaw Anders' army to the Middle East, there were still hundreds of thousands of Poles left in the Soviet Union. A small group of Polish Communists organized what they called a Polish Patriots Union and petitioned Soviet Premier Josef Stalin to form a new Polish infantry division. This time, the units would be under strict Soviet control. For Poles left in the Soviet Union, joining a newly forming army offered the only hope of getting out of the camps and prisons in which they were detained and leaving the Soviet Union altogether.

News about the formation of a new Polish army spread fast and recruits began to arrive at the small town of Sielce on the Oka River. Some of them had been officially 'released' from internment, while others without papers gave false names. Despite problems with training, accommodation, food and equipment and large differences in age and military education, the 1st Polish Infantry Division, known as the Tadeusz Kosciuszko Division, was formed in June of 1943. To lead it, Stalin chose Lieutenant-Colonel Zygmunt Berling, a Polish officer who had collaborated with the NKVD after 1939 and deserted from Anders' army during its evacuation to the Middle East. Sure of his compliance, the Soviets made him general and division commander.

After three months of training, the Kosciuszko Division was declared to be ready for service at the front. It was given the task of assisting Russian divisions in breaking through strong German fortifications at Lenino. Although this new Polish Army was ill prepared to confront the well-trained and well-equipped German forces, its political leaders and its officers, who were almost exclusively Russians, were eager to please Stalin.

The Kosciuszko Division went to battle on October 12, 1943. The Poles fought valiantly, capturing the village of Polzuchy, but after two days of intense fighting they had to be withdrawn from the front because of extremely high losses. Entering the battle with 11,444 men, the division lost 502 killed, 1,776 wounded, and 663 missing in action — twenty-five per cent of its original strength!

Infantry units train in Ukraine, May 1944

Volunteers from the 1st Mortar Company of the 1st Infantry Division march during their training.

One of the last training sessions — a river-crossing manoeuvre — before going to battle.

A growing number of displaced and deported Poles joined what came to be known as the Polish People's Army. By the end of the war, its ranks had swelled to the point that two separate armies had been created. Altogether, ten Polish divisions fought under Soviet control, participating in the liberation of Poland, Czechoslovakia and the Battle of Berlin.

Lublin, Poland, July 1944. Poles welcome freedom from German occupation with the Polish flag.

Soldiers of the Polish People's Army before they parade through the streets of Lublin.

Soldiers of the 1st Infantry Division battle for control of Prague, Czechoslovakia, September 1944

Soldiers of the 2nd Polish Corps in Khanaqin, Iraq. At right Mieczyslaw Szczecinski. *Mieczyslaw Szczecinski*

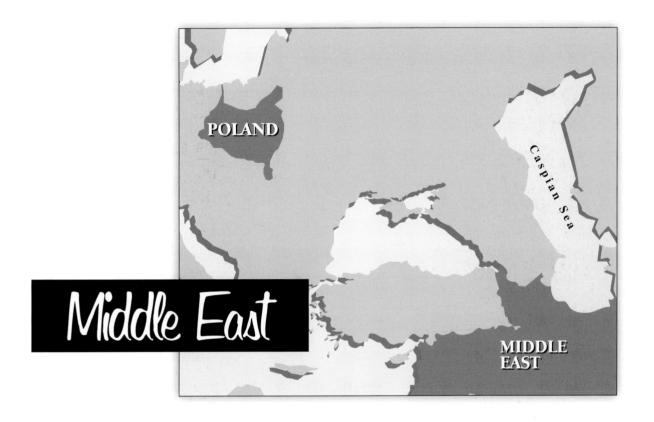

Middle East

The Polish units that left the Soviet Union in 1942 went first to Iran and then to Iraq, where a new training centre was formed. They were joined there by the Carpathian Brigade, fresh from the Libyan campaign, and in this way the Polish 2nd Army Corps was formed.

The first transport of Polish troops and civilians arrives from Krasnovodsk, Russia, in Pahlevi, Iran.

Soldiers of the Polish 2nd Corps.

The evacuation of the Polish Army, under the command of General Wladyslaw Anders, took place from March to August 1942. Altogether, about 114,000 Polish soldiers and civilians were transported from Russia to the Iranian port of Pahlevi.

The new arrivals received a warm welcome from both representatives of the British Army and from their Iranian hosts, who apparently were fully informed about the gruelling experiences undergone by the Poles.

From Pahlevi, the Polish troops were moved into Iraq. The British Army intended to make full use of this new-found manpower and a training centre was set up in the desert at Quizil Ribat. Living in tents, the emerging army underwent a rigorous period of training in the use of British military equipment.

These Polish troops from the depths of Russian Siberia were joined by the Carpathian Brigade, which had fought in Libya in 1941. They were also joined by Poles who had escaped from Poland through Rumania and Hungary. In May 1942, the Polish 2nd Army Corps was formed.

In the autumn of 1943, the high command decided to use Polish troops on the Italian front. They were moved from Iraq to Palestine. They continued their military training in Palestine as well as in the highlands of Syria, preparing themselves for imminent combat.

At the end of December 1943, the Polish 2nd Army Corps was moved by way of Egypt to Italy, where it fought with distinction in the battles of Monte Cassino, Ancona and Bologna.

There were a large number of civilians who had arrived with the Polish Army at Pahlevi. They settled on the outskirts of Teheran, where they organized their own community. Polish signs for kitchens, laundries, schools and tailors appeared everywhere. Polish shops and cafés with Polish waiters sprang up almost overnight. There were even actors and musicians from the Warsaw theatres. They had taken refuge in Lwow during the siege of Warsaw and were then caught up in the wave of deportation. Their performances became a regular feature of Polish emigré life in Teheran.

Iraq, Qaiyara, February 2, 1943. "New" soldiers of the 1st Carpathian Brigade take the oath in front of Chaplin W. Judycki.

"A whole new Polish Army is strung out hundreds of miles across the Near East — thousands of tough fighting troops released from Soviet prison camps and sent down through Russia to join the British (March, 1942).

They include airmen, sailors, soldiers, engineers, railway troops, and special formations, all in uniform.... For nearly a month now they have been pouring through Persia by railway and mountain road....

The Russians sent them by ship to a little Caspian port, Pahlevi, where Britain's Tenth Army was working at short notice to receive them.

Pahlevi was 3 ft. deep in snow, so shelter had to be found. Seats were ripped from the town's biggest cinema, and every empty house was requisitioned.

Army rations were rushed up by lorry. Live sheeps were brought from local shepherds. Medical supplies, warm clothing, and thousands of blankets were concentrated. Yet, even so, the first contingent was three times as big as had been planned for. They proved tough, lean men, in fine physical condition, and mad keen to get within fighting distance of Germans.

They were wearing British battle dress, and their morale was so high that they right away organized an impromptu concert in their cinema-lodging....

Hundreds of the women belonged to the Polish Women's Auxiliary Force....

Some married couples were reunited in Pahlevi after two years' separation....

The whole of the first big contingent has been cleared from Pahlevi. Their numbers cannot be mentioned, but the force is an important addition to the armies fighting for democracy."

Alexander Clifford, *Daily Mail* correspondent, on the formation of the Polish Army in the Middle East — later the Polish 2nd Corps. April 24, 1942

Soldiers celebrate their graduation from military school and training at Qauyara, March 1943.

"Vojtek" was sold to a group of Polish soldiers as an orphan cub in Iran in 1942. As a member of the 22nd Company, he took part in the Italian campaign, helping with unloading heavy artillery shells and boxes of ammunition. After demobilization, Vojtek found a haven at the Zoological Garden in Edinburgh, Scotland. He died in 1984. *Sikorski Museum*

Army manoeuvres in the Iraqi desert.

162

A Polish troop camp in Palestine. The place, names and scenery changed but the tents were always the same.

"Of the various Allied contingents which the armies in the Middle East now comprise, the Poles are by far the biggest. The large draft which arrived three months ago from Russia raised them at once to the rank of a small army, complete with all arms and auxiliary services, including a most useful women's corps, which supplies cooks, orderlies, and so on. Before that there had been but one Polish unit in the Middle East — the brigade which took such a gallant part in the defence of Tobruk. Now that brigade is only one of many.

The Polish troops are quartered in a series of camps which spread themselves over 50 miles of open Palestinian country, where the sea breezes temper the summer heat. I found all arms hard at work training and accustoming themselves to the new British equipment; this equipment is not yet complete, but it is coming along by degrees. There are whole units here which fought against the Germans in Poland; but a fair percentage of the men recruited from the Polish civilian population deported to Russia has not yet seen service. Whether veterans or recruits, their physical standard is of the highest; they look workmanlike and as hard as nails, and their discipline is noticeably good.

This is going to be an army to be reckoned with."

The Times correspondent in Palestine on the Polish Army in the Middle East. August 6, 1942

163

The 2nd Corps unit parades with its new Allied Sherman tanks. Palestine, November 1943

The Polish 2nd Corps on parade in Palestine, July 24, 1943

Members of the future Polish Women's Auxiliary Corps receive their first meal shortly after arriving in the recruiting centre on the Volga steppes, Russia.

Women Soldiers of the 2nd Polish Corps

In military uniform, from left, Zofia Grudzienska, Iga Zymanek and Aleksandra Dabrowska (Markiewicz). *Aleksandra Markiewicz*

After long negotiations with the Soviet government, General Wladyslaw Anders created the Polish Women's Auxiliary Corps — the PSK. He had two motives in doing so. First, he was intent on saving the greatest number of women from the prisons and detention camps of the Soviet Union. Second, he wanted to secure the greatest number of auxiliary workers to assist his growing army.

The women who entered the auxiliary were on the same footing as the men. They took up their work in hospitals, canteens, cook-houses, laundries and offices. Many took the opportunity to study in the evenings in order to pass military and technical tests.

Along with the thousands of Polish deportees arriving from the far reaches of Russia came huge numbers of children. They were half starved, debilitated by disease, and decimated by epidemics.

They required a great deal of care and were eventually taken with the Army when it moved into Iran. Members of the PSK were given the task of teaching these children, nursing the sick, and combating disease. This work continued even after the army arrived in Pahlevi.

The PSK followed the Polish 2nd Corps in its advance through Italy, playing an important supporting role by managing hospitals, canteens, communications services and transportation.

Through the Arctic wastes, the Siberian tundra and the Western Asiatic steppes, through prisons and detention camps, amid humiliation, hunger and misery, Polish women carried on bravely.

A Polish woman in one of the military camps in Russia. They were quartered in tents as temperatures dropped to lows of -50° C.

Worn-out clothes have been exchanged for warm uniforms that gave the PSK the nickname "Penguins."

Spring 1942. Left: In Krasnovodsk, their last day in Russia, female soldiers wait to leave for Pahlevi, Iran. Right: On their first day in Pahlevi, the women are greeted by Colonel Jastrzebski. *Aleksandra Markiewicz*

Polish women receive their army uniforms. *Sikorski Museum*

170

Left: At the entrance to school, Jenin. Right: On the beach, Tel Aviv, 1942. *Aleksandra Markiewicz*

Polish women train in their new uniforms. *Sikorski Museum*

During the Italian campaign, the 316 and 317 PSK Transport Companies accounted for 43,339 trips, used 342,370 gallons of gasoline and drove 3,600,608 miles.
They delivered a total of 183,503 tons of ammunition, food, gas, spare parts and construction materials.

PSK transport soldiers take a driving course. They had to know how to take care of their vehicles, repair small problems and often load and unload them.

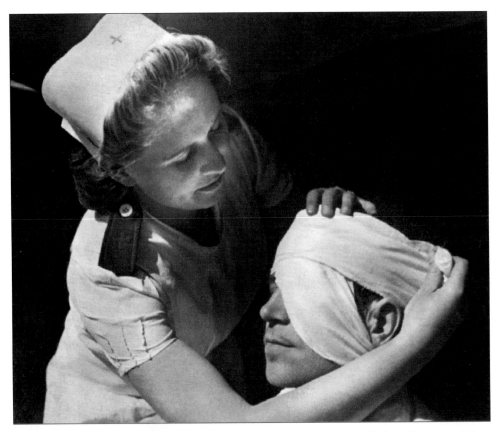

A nurse bandages a wounded soldier. Nurses changed dressings, washed and fed the ill, gave medicine and, most importantly, smiled and offered cheerful words to keep the soldiers in good spirits.

Everyone wants to know the latest news from the fronts around the world.

After the defeat of the enemy, together with the victors of Monte Cassino, Ancona and Bologna, members of the PSK receive their well-earned awards.

General Morgan, accompanied by General Wladyslaw Anders, commander of the Polish 2nd Corps, visits the 316 Transport Company.

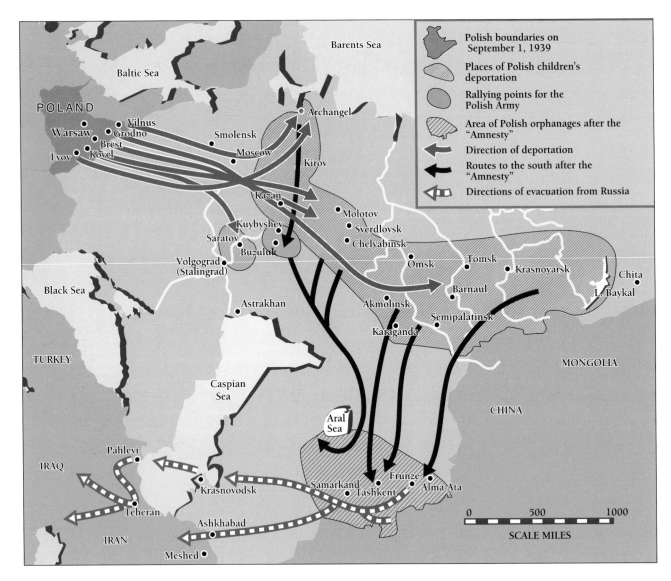

The routes of Polish children's deportation.

Polish Children in Exile

It is estimated that 380,000 Polish children were deported to the Soviet Union after September 1939. Those who could accompanied the thousands of volunteers and civilians who joined the Polish Army forming under General Wladyslaw Anders.

"Mothers headed with their children towards the army camps, or knowing they are too weak to survive the trip they parted with them, seeing that this is the only way their children will get help and be taken care of by the Army....

The influx of children into the army centers was large.... A majority of them had no documents, nor any referral slips.... Girls with close-cropped hair because of typhoid and with rib cages collapsed, were difficult to distinguish from boys except by their clothing.... Hundreds of these little victims did not live to see a better day. Dying, they did not complain about parting from a life that had treated them so cruelly. Only those who had a close relative with them did not want to die but begged to be saved....

During the summer of 1942, a total number of 77,200 soldiers and 37,300 civilians, including 15,000 children, were evacuated from Krasnovodosk, on the Caspian Sea, to the Persian port of Pahlevi.

Exhaustion and the sudden change in living conditions caused diseases to break out. The Saint Lazarus Order of Monks offered their cemetery for the burial of the dead, but it filled so quickly that a new cemetery had to be assigned especially for Poles. Two thousand found rest in it. This cemetery differed from others in that it had very many crosses marked 'NN', for the nameless dead.... On the gravestones of 400 Polish children are inscriptions such as 'Here rests Johnny,' or simply 'Henry, age 6, died....' Over two hundred of these graves bear no names. No one could tell whom these children belonged to or where they had been born....

None of us could forget that we represented only a very small percentage of all the Polish people deported to Russia between 1939 and 1941, and that after the last transport of civilians and military had arrived (to Pahlavi), at least one million of our countrymen, along with their children, remained dependent upon the good or ill will of the Soviet NKVD."

L. Krolikowski in *Stolen Childhood, A Saga Of Polish War Children*

Young PSK recruits, exhausted but saved, after their arrival across the Caspian Sea to Iran at the port of Pahlevi.

Polish girls become Girl Guides in Iran. They were happy, safe, dressed and, most importantly, not hungry anymore.

182

Polish children accompanying those arriving at Pahlevi no longer needed the protection of the Polish Army. Civilian and military schools for boys and girls were rapidly organized. From Iran they were later moved to Palestine and Egypt.

Schools for girls were first set up at Geder, then in Jenin, before they found a permanent location in Nazareth. In July 1947, these schools were transferred to England. Most Palestinians were very helpful and friendly; some even began to learn Polish. Even so, the gym uniforms and short-sleeved army uniforms worn by girl students offended many devout Muslims. As a result, very strict rules were introduced regarding trips to the city and exercises on outdoor fields.

There is a story told that during one bus excursion to Syria, an elderly Arab woman attempted to buy two blond girls from the tour guide. She did not know anything about the Polish school and thought that the girls all belonged to the guide! The population around Nazareth, however, was familiar with the Polish school there and it was used to foreigners, having been acclimatized by the presence of a British police station and paratroop brigade.

Smaller and younger Polish children evacuated from Russia were sent to several refugee camps outside Palestine. The largest group went to Africa, where Great Britain had granted them hospitality in her colonies. Smaller groups went to India, Mexico and New Zealand. In India, the Maharajah of Nawanagar built a seashore camp in Balacheri to accommodate 5,000 children. Two other local rulers provided for another 10,000. Most of these camps included school rooms where the children learned English, Polish and the language of their host county.

General Wladyslaw Anders with two cadets, Jan Gasztold, left, and Jan Swirkowski. *J. Gasztold*

For boys aged thirteen to seventeen who had been evacuated from Russia, a special Military Cadet School was established in Palestine and Egypt. The school was located in the desert, first at Bash-it, then Qyastina and finally at Barbara, where it remained until it was transferred to England in 1947 and dissolved in the following year.

This cadet academy was modelled on the School of Knights that had been created in 18th-century Poland, and also on the cadet schools that existed in Poland until 1939. In addition to their own insignia, the cadets wore the insignia of the Polish 3rd Carpathian Division, which adopted them. They were especially favoured by General Wladyslaw Anders, the commander of the

July 1943: Last parade in front of General Wladyslaw Sikorski. On July 4, 1943, a few seconds after takeoff from Gibraltar, Sikorski's plane plummetted into the sea. The General and all of the other passengers were killed. *A. Markiewicz*

Polish 2nd Corps, who inscribed their Memorial Book with the words: "Remember, my boys, that 'Polish Cadet' is a synonym for honesty, bravery and honour."

When they attained military age, more than one hundred of these cadets were transferred to the Polish 2nd Corps in Italy. They took part in the Italian campaign and participated in the battles of Monte Cassino, Piedimonte, Ancona and Bologna.

They established a reputation for exemplary bravery, earning many decorations for valour. Many of them sacrificed their young lives and their graves can be found in every Polish military cemetery in Italy. Another 340 cadets were transferred to the Polish Air Force and Navy.

With the end of the war, Poland found itself under Communist domination. These young people, who had already experienced Communist rule in the Soviet Union, were unwilling to return to the land of their birth. Instead, they scattered to whatever countries were willing to take them in. Many settled in Great Britain, Canada and the United States.

Day by day, young soldiers, well fed after years of starvation, are reviving and becoming physically strong.

Soldiers of the 3rd Carpathian Rifle Division blow up enemy bunkers during the Battle of Monte Cassino.

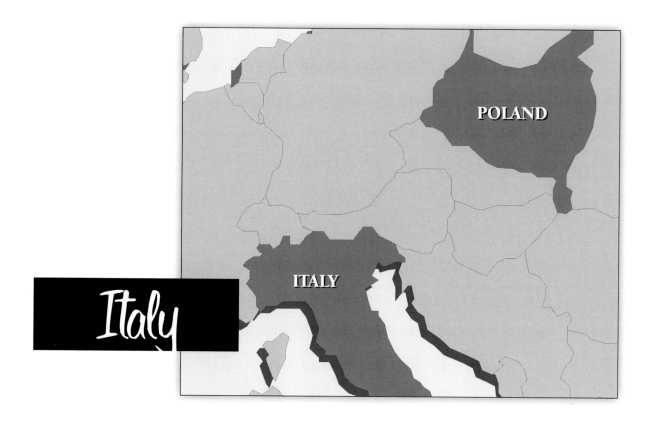

Italy

"The Second Polish Corps is now fighting in Italy under Lieut.-General Wladyslaw Anders.
The Carpathian and Kresowa Divisions form part of the corps. These divisions consist of men who escaped after
the German invasion of Poland. The Carpathian Brigade earlier had distinguished itself in the defense of Tobruk.
The Polish troops have been rigorously trained in Persia and Iraq."

Communique issued from Allied Headquarters in Italy. February 16, 1944

187

Soldiers of the Polish 2nd Corps in front of the pyramids. They came to Egypt from Palestine to finish their training before leaving for Italy. At centre is Mieczyslaw Szczecinski. *Mieczyslaw Szczecinski*

In mid-December 1943, the Polish 2nd Corps was transported from Palestine, via Egypt, to the Italian Front, where it came under the command of the British 8th Army. Composed of the 3rd and 5th Infantry divisions, an Armoured Brigade, artillery groups and a special corps of supporting units, it totalled 55,000 officers and men.

Its single most important contribution in the Italian campaign was at the battle of Monte Cassino, which opened the road to Rome. The system of fortifications around Monte Cassino was key to the entire German defence of Italy. The Allies had attacked it three times already when, on May 11, the Polish 2nd Corps had its turn. Fierce fighting and repeated German counterattacks brought the first Polish assault to a standstill. On May 16, the Poles took control of several important positions on the slopes of the hill a monastery sat atop. After a flanking manoeuvre, the Poles gained more ground. The monastery was finally taken on May 18, 1944, and the nearby town of Piedimonte fell on May 25.

In mid-June, the 2nd Corps began operations along the Adriatic coast. From July 17 to 20, it captured Ancona, an important supply post. This was followed by heavy battles against elite Nazi units in extremely difficult mountain conditions on the Misa, Cesano, Metauro, Foglia and Senio Rivers. Fighting along the Senio River lasted from January until April 1945.

In the last battles of the Italian campaign, the 2nd Corps initiated an attack in the direction of Bologna on April 9, 1945. It captured Imola on the 15th and stormed Bologna itself on the 21st. The war in Europe ended a few weeks later.

188

Routes of the 2nd Polish Corps in the Italian Campaign.

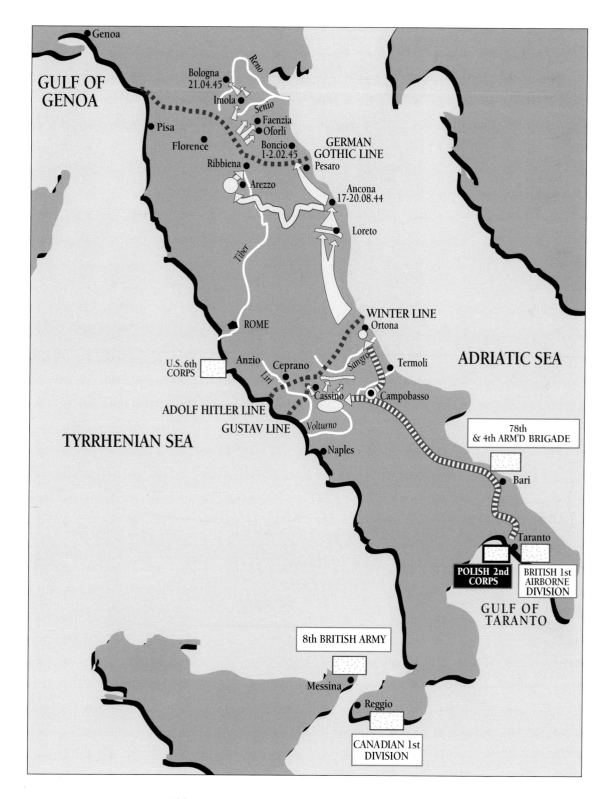

Battlefields

Concentration of
Armed Forces

Actions and battles

March routes

An assault group of the Carpathian Battalion, Sangro. Second from left in the first row is Stanislaw Tebinka.

"Fighting throughout the night against odds of two, and three, to one, Polish Commandos attached to the Eighth Army saved British gun emplacements overlooking the Sangro River.

Today, I can tell some of the story of how much of the Eighth Army's reconnaissance patrolling was done by a small number of these Polish Commandos, trained in Britain. That was their primary task, but when occupying a mountain village and attacked by German Alpine troops, they beat off the enemy after being completely cut off and surrounded.

Behind the Poles were British field-gun emplacements, undoubtedly the enemy's objective.

Early in December, 1943, the Poles were ordered from their base town to the Eighth Army front. After a two-day journey over bad mountain roads they reached the little village of Capracotta, high in the Apennines, which for days was to be their headquarters.

Capracotta, destroyed by the Germans as they retreated, was the Eighth Army's last outpost. Only the River Sangro separated them from the Germans, and it was the Commandos' task to pay frequent 'visits' to the enemy to find out their positions and strength.

They got to work at once. Night raids were the order, but the Poles found that they were impossible. The Nazis had laid down hundreds of mines, and the patrols had to be carried out in daylight.

On December 14, a large patrol led by their commanding officer set off on what they described as a 'log walk' into Nazi positions. They crossed the river safely, and some distance on the other side surprised a German party in a fortified house.

The Poles got to within 25 yards of the 'fort' before they were discovered, and the Germans opened fire with a machine-gun.

A sniper shot one of the Commandos 'covering' the patrol. Braving the point-blank enemy fire an officer and an N.C.O. carried the wounded man to safety, and the patrol got back without further casualties.

On this sector the Poles claim to be the first to cross the Sangro."

The Evening Standard. February 9, 1944

190

December 25, 1943, Francavilla, North of Taranto.
Shortly after arriving back on European soil, Polish
soldiers from the 3rd Carpathian Brigade celebrate
Christmas Day with Italian children and their families.
From left: S. Ratajczak, S. Bukowinski, A. Czernicki
and Henryk Starczewski. *Henryk Starczewski*

In the ruins of the monastery at Monte Cassino.

192

Battle of Monte Cassino

The monastery at Monte Cassino after the battle.

Monte Cassino overlooks the major road running through the southern part of Italy. The Germans had fortified the monastery on top of the hill, and built bunkers around it, making it the linchpin of their "Gustav" system of defences. From this vantage point they controlled all road traffic to and from Rome. The taking of Monte Cassino meant breaking the Gustav line and opening the road to Rome.

The Australians, the British and the Canadians had already made several unsuccessful attempts on the fortress. In May of 1944, another assault was ordered on the monastery, this time by the Polish 2nd Corps under the command of General Wladyslaw Anders. Flanked by the Canadian 1st Corps, the Polish 2nd Corps moved into action.

For a week, the monastery was bombarded and shelled by artillery and tanks. Polish sappers built an access road that would allow tanks to move further up the mountain sides. When the bombardment stopped, the troops moved forward, slowly working their way up the hill. As they overcame German defensive positions and demined the slopes, the sappers took the brunt of the German fire, incurring very heavy casualties.

The final assault was fast and fierce. In the final stages of the battle, the Poles would throw hand grenades and then follow up with a bayonet charge. Despite heavy losses, the Polish assault persisted and on May 18, 1944, the fortress was captured.

It was the single greatest Polish victory of the Second World War. It did not come cheaply: more than 1,000 men died on the battlefield and 3,000 were wounded.

Tanks on the way to attack positions take sappers to clean the route and disarm the mines put down by the Germans.

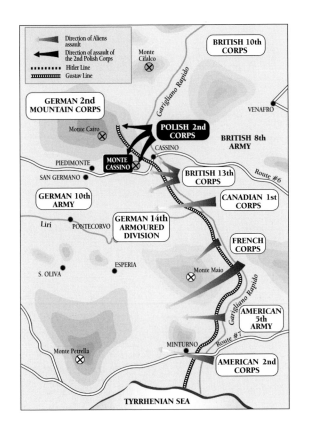

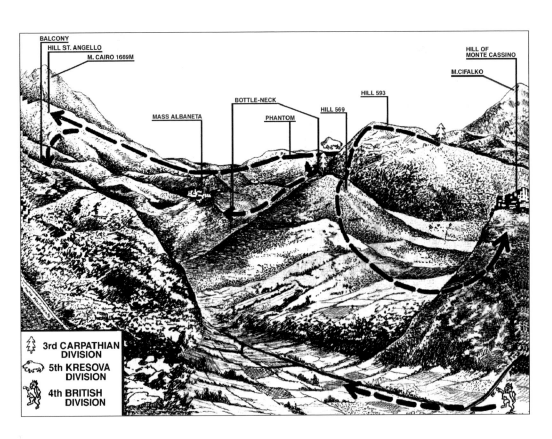

The battle fields of Monte Cassino.

"The Poles had much to do with the final stages of the campaign in the Cassino area..... It was here that the Poles avenged the five years of German occupation of their country.

The Poles flung themselves against positions that were considered impregnable — and took them. They had, it appears, the hardest task yet assigned to troops on the Eighth Army front...."

Correspondent of *The Yorkshire Post* on the fall of Cassino. May 18, 1944

The cemetery in San Vittore. Before battle, empty graves are waiting.

Soldiers and special Italian patrols collect the bodies of those who lost their lives in battle. Some died on the stretchers, when help was so close.

A last farewell to fallen comrades.

The crew of Lieutenant Bialecki was the first to die in the Battle of Monte Cassino.

General Wladyslaw Anders and General Keighthley of the British 78th Division study maps before the final battle.

"Polish troops in an all-out attack against German strong points around the Monastery
Hill and Cassino area today drove down from the hills towards Highway Six.
I was with the Carpathians, those magnificent fighters who made history
at Gazala and Tobruk. They were the spearhead of the attack....
Polish infantry attacked on the rugged mountain feature 1,000 yards from their starting line.
After a sharp, fierce clash, they captured their first objective in two hours.
Then came the most bitter battle of the day, the fight for Mt. Albaneta, a
key point of the German defenses around the Benedictine Monastery.
There were desperate hand-to-hand clashes. The Poles achieved almost impossible
feats. At one point they had to swarm up a sheer face of the mountain on rope ladders...."

Correspondent Graham Beamish of *The Daily Telegraph* on the Polish attack west of Cassino. May 17, 1944

Commandos charge up a hill under a smoke screen.

It isn't often possible to take a lunch break.

Soldiers of the 3rd Carpathian Brigade put heavy mortar into firing position.

"Magnificent fighting both by the British and Polish troops made the capture possible.

The Poles, after desperate fighting across Phantom Ridge, went on to wage a bloody battle for Mass Albaneta, the key position.

Scrambling their way up steep slopes, they fought gallantly towards the fortified house known as 'the fortress' which once was the home of the Benedictine monks.

It cost many lives to capture it, but the Poles stormed the heights and the Huns realised that it was all up. The Germans came out with their hands up because they knew they were at the mercy of an enemy who hated them.

The next day the Poles massed for the all-important final desperate assault on the monastery itself.

It was a fantastic battle with Polish tanks, supported by anti-tank guns, standing in the front line smashing at pillboxes.

Then the Poles came down out of the hills to join hands with the British troops, and the pride of the German Army, the First Parachute Division, was trapped."

Correspondent of T*he Daily Mirror* on the fall of Cassino.
May 18, 1944

Special net camouflages artillery shells and ammunition boxes.

An artillery position.

The last "inspection." General Wladyslaw Anders in the temporary cemetery after the Battle of Monte Cassino.

"Of the many cables and congratulations, the greatest recognition came from Marshal
Alexander saying: 'Soldiers of the 2nd Polish Corps, I can assure you sincerely:
should I be given any choice of any soldiers whom I would like to command, I
would choose you Poles. I salute you'."

S. Baluk in *Poles On The Fronts Of World War II*

Dead and wounded soldiers of the 5th Kresowa Infantry Division.
During the Italian Campaign, a total of 11,198 soldiers of the 2nd Corps were injured or killed.

"Cassino and Monastery Hill, which have resisted the allied attack for four months, fell this morning as the result of the combined efforts of the Polish Corps operating on the heights and the British troops in the plain...."

Correspondent of *The Times* at Allied Headquarters, Italy. May 18, 1944

"Trudging through Cassino at 5:30 this evening I saw the Union Jack and the Polish flag hoisted over the ruins of Cassino's monastery. That symbolised the defeat of the cream of Germany's armies."

Daily Express correspondent John Redfern on the fall of Cassino. May 18, 1944

At 10 a.m. on May 18, 1944, the red-and-white Polish flag is hoisted over the ruins of the captured Monte Cassino Monastery.

Before action at Loretto. Lieutenant Henryk Starczewski is at right. *Henryk Starczewski*

Polish troops in Loretto, the historical city for centuries visited by Polish noblemen and pilgrims.

"The break through of the Poles at Ancona seems to have been extremely well handled. It was important that the German line should be broken and armour sent through in force before the Germans were able to get their guns and heavy material back across the Esino River, which runs out into the sea about eight miles west of the port. If they had been able to do this they might have held up the Poles on the Esino and kept Ancona under their fire, thus making it difficult to develop it as a supply base. To all appearances this has been prevented....

More than 2,000 prisoners had been counted yesterday, and the official report speaks of Polish tanks relentlessly pursuing the retreating enemy. It is known that Polish troops reached the sea well west of Ancona, so it is highly probable that they have captured the bulk of the German artillery concentrated in a valley behind the high promontory which shields Ancona from the south....

General Anders has thus satisfactorily carried out the task allotted to the Polish Corps by General Alexander when it took over from the Indians on the Pescara River a month or so ago. Since then it has advanced 75 miles, stubbornly overcoming tenacious German resistance...."

Correspondent of *The Times* on the capture of the town and port of Ancona by the Polish 2nd Corps. July 18, 1944

Victory.

During the advance on Ancona, soldiers reload ammunition and clean guns.

"The Poles in the capture of Ancona virtually destroyed the German 278th Division, one of two
which had been allotted to the defense of the port, and captured much valuable material.
The Poles are now reported to have reached the Esino River on a front of about six miles up to the
mouth.... The Poles are now beginning to encounter some resistance in their pursuit of the enemy,
but they have already advanced far enough to prevent the Germans from bringing heavy artillery fire
to bear on Ancona and interfering with our use of the port...."

Correspondent of *The Times* on the capture of the town and port of Ancona by the Polish 2nd Corps. July 20, 1944

On the Gothic Line, close to the Metauro River, tanks and infantry units change position.

Building the bridge in Rocca San Casciano. The winter weather in Apennines made the work of Polish sappers even more difficult.

"Polish troops of the Eighth Army have captured Imola and are approaching the Sillaro River, on their right, the Eighth Army bridgehead over the river has been considerably strengthened. South of Lake Comacchio heavy fighting continues.

An earlier 'REUTER' dispatch said:

'Troops of the Polish Second Corps were battling with fanatical German paratroops in the streets of the town and around the railway station, the Caproni aeroplane factory, and a munition works. The enemy was using the cathedral spire as an observation post'."

Communique from Allied Headquarters, Mediterranean, on the battle on the Rimini-Bologna highway. April 15, 1945

Polish soldiers captured Bologna.

"Troops of the Polish Second Corps
entered Bologna yesterday along the
Via Emilia."

Correspondent of *The Manchester Guardian.*
April 22, 1945

German prisoners of war. They fought desperately for Bologna, but had to surrender.

General Bronislaw Rakowski presents to General Wladyslaw Anders a captured German paratroopers' flag after Bologna was captured by the Polish 2nd Corps on April 21, 1945

The citizens of Bologna greet their Polish liberators.

"My warmest congratulations to the troops which have seized
this vital military objective after a winter's campaign that has
presented almost insuperable obstacles in terrain, weather,
and fanatical enemy resistance."

Message from Field Marshal Sir Harold Alexander, Supreme Allied Commander,
Mediterranean, on the capture of Bologna by Polish troops of the 8th Army.
April 21, 1945

General Zygmunt Szyszko-Bohusz and General Klemens Rudnicki enter the town of Bologna.

"The Poles are stationed along the Adriatic coast, from Bari up to the plain of the Po. They have relieved many British troops who have been demobilized or withdrawn.

This has been welcome from our point of view, since the strain of the multifarious duties which have had to be carried out with depleted forces has been considerable.

It has already been announced that it is British policy to encourage Polish troops to return to their country. There can, however, be no question of compelling them to do so against their will. Nor can they be turned off to become 'displaced persons.' Even if humanity were not taken into account, it is not desired to add to the displaced and masterless population of Europe.

But humanitarian feeling does, and must, affect the British attitude because so deep a debt of gratitude is owed to these troops. In the first instance, they joined our standards when our military affairs were neither prosperous nor promising. They were well led; in fact some considered General Anders the best corps commander in Italy. They did not use their peculiar status as the biggest allied force attached to the British Army to make bargains about how they should be employed, but took the rough with the smooth and got at least their share of the rough."

Correspondent of *The Times* in tribute to the Polish 2nd Corps in Italy. February 18, 1946

General Wladyslaw Anders addresses the Women's Auxilliary Corps with the words: "We will go from Italy through Great Britain — and then through any land we will have to — until we reach the independent Poland we were fighting for."

The Polish 2nd Corps remained in Italy after the German surrender. Then, on May 23, 1946, the British decision to demobilize the Polish Armed Forces was made public.

Those serving in the Polish forces refused to accept this order. There was something heroic in the massive refusal to recognize and accept the dramatic reality of the fact that Poland had been handed over to Soviet control. From a historical perspective, no precedents for such an attitude existed in any modern army.

Despite British displeasure, numerous statements by General Wladyslaw Anders and by Polish political leaders in exile stressed repeatedly that they would not give up their efforts to oppose the political order that had been imposed upon their homeland. They would continue to fight for Poland's independence, even if their armies were demobilized by the British authorities.

U.S. General Dwight D. Eisenhower (centre) inspects the Polish 1st Armoured Division in Holland, November 29, 1944. Second from right is General Stanislaw Maczek.

Low Countries

After its brilliant victory at the Falaise Gap, the Polish 1st Armoured Division continued its advance through Normandy, eventually pushing into the Low Countries. Driving the Germans back through Belgium and Holland, the Poles took part in the liquidation of a German bridgehead in the region of Skadla. The Poles spent the next three months waging a hard-fought campaign in Holland that culminated in a victorious attack on Moerdijk.

Soldiers of the 1st Armoured Division during the operations in the area of Merxplas-Tilburg.

When the Battle for Normandy came to an end, the 1st Armoured Division, under the command of General Stanislaw Maczek, was assigned to the Low Countries. It advanced through Rouen, Pas-De-Calais and to the southern part of Belgium. The division crossed the French border with Belgium on September 6, 1944, and continued against fierce German opposition at Ypres, Ghent and Antwerp.

The division's first engagements on Dutch soil began on September 28, and by October it had liberated the town of Breda in a tactical manoeuvre that left most of the city untouched by fighting. As a mark of their joy at being liberated, the people of Breda conferred honorary citizenship on all soldiers of the 1st Armoured Division, and renamed one of their streets Poolsche Weg.

The 1st Armoured Division continued its campaign in Holland with a successful engagement at Moerdijk, an assault on Groningen, and the landing of paratroops at Arnhem.

England, 1944. Paratroopers of the Polish Paratroop Brigade receive last instructions from Group Captain Maurice Newan before taking off for Holland. *IWM - M.H.1962*

Members of the Paratroop Brigade with their "bicycle" before going to action in Operation Market. *Sikorski Museum*

The Polish Independent Paratroop Brigade was created in England in 1941 and trained there until 1944 under the command of General Stanislaw Sosabowski. Together with the British 1st Airborne Division, it took part in the largest airborne operation of the war — Operation Market — at Arnhem and Driel.

The objective was to capture and secure the bridge across the Rhine at Arnhem. This would give Allied armies a way of crossing the river as they advanced into the very heart of Germany. The Germans expected the attack, and prepared a powerful defence. As a result, the paratroops were put into a hopeless position. They made the jump behind the German lines without the heavy anti-tank equipment they needed. In addition, a shortage of boats meant that only a portion of the brigade actually crossed the river. As a result, both the Polish Paratroop Brigade and the British 1st Airborne Division suffered heavy losses.

It was an operation "one bridge too far."

Paratroops fire three-inch mortars on enemy positions across the Rhine River on September 20, 1944. *IWM - B.U.1099*

Men of the 1st Paratroop Battalion take cover in a small crater. *IWM - B.U.1167*

"It is requested that you will forward to the Commander of the Polish Independent Paratroop Brigade Group my appreciation of their services whilst they were under my command for 'Operation Market.'

The Glider element of the Brigade landed on 19th September, and were with us throughout the battle. The Paratroop Brigade Group has landed on the South bank of the River Rhine opposite our bridge-head on 21st September....

The losses sustained both before and during the evacuation were heavy. It may, however, be a satisfaction to know that these losses were not in vain and that the name of the Polish Independent Paratroop Brigade Group will be linked to that of the 1st British Airborne Division in connection with the memorable battle at Arnhem."

Major General R.E. Urquart of the 1st Airborne Division to General Kazimierz Sosnkowski, Commander-in-Chief of the Polish forces, on the action at Arnhem by the Polish Parachute Brigade. October 2, 1944

Men of the 3rd Platoon of Independent Paratroop Brigade after the battle at Osterbreek. They were the only survivors of their platoon of 30 people. Standing at left is Jan Towarnicki. *Jan Towarnicki*

General Stanislaw Sosabowski, commander of the 1st Independent Airborne Brigade, during the operation near Driel. He strongly criticized the action at Arnhem, and later was dismissed from his rank as a commander.

The morning after the battle at Driel; it feels good to shave again. *Sikorski Museum*

"During recent weeks the Poles have been fighting under extremely difficult conditions, and have established an outstanding reputation by their accomplishments....

As stated last week by General Crerar, 'Every demand ever made on those troops has been met. Every task has been completed, no matter how bitter the enemy's defense or how unfavorable the natural conditions. With such officers and men military success and final victory can never be in doubt.'

In all the fighting of the First Canadian Army during the past three months the Polish troops have set the finest of military standards."

General Henry Crerar, Commander-in-Chief of the 1st Canadian Army, on the Polish 1st Armoured Division in Holland (from the Canadian Army newspaper *Maple Leaf*). November 1, 1944

A Polish soldier shares his meal with Dutch children.

A trooper of the Polish 1st Armoured Division stands in front of a sign made by the citizens of Breda: "Thank you, Poles." November 1944. *IWM - M.H.1396.*

Field Marshal Sir Bernard Montgomery decorates Colonel T. Majewski of the Polish 1st Armoured Division, November 25, 1944

"In those areas of Belgium and Holland which I have recently visited I found the Poles and the people of the liberated towns and villages getting on extremely well together. It was an amazing experience to enter places in both countries and see what joy the Poles brought by their victory. I saw people standing in the doorways of their homes, damaged only perhaps an hour before in the fighting, throwing flowers and handing fruit to the troops and cheering themselves hoarse. In one Flanders village I remember going into a shop to make a small purchase. The proprietor behind the counter said to me: 'We have had to billet our enemies the Germans again and again. We are very glad they have been driven out now. Perhaps you will send us a Polish soldier and we will be only too glad to give him a free billet'."

Speech of Colonel Harold Mitchell in the House of Commons during debate on the war and the international situation. September 29, 1944

Berlin, July 1945. The Brandenburg Gate, surrounded by wrecked buildings, after the final battle for Berlin. *IWM - CL.3229*

Germany

Polish soldiers were in action from the first day of the war and their efforts continued unabated until its last day. When the war came to German soil, Polish units were there. Ironically, they entered Germany aligned with the two sides that were emerging to define the shape of the post-war world. In the West, Polish divisions fought alongside the British Army. In the East, the Polish People's Army fought under Soviet control.

Spring, 1945. Polish sappers work to prepare bridges in time for tanks to cross over.

The Yalta Conference had already foreshadowed a post-war division of Europe in which Poland would be consigned to Soviet domination. This made Poland the only ally to actually lose its independence despite its participation in the war effort.

Despite their heavy losses and an increasingly uncertain future for their country, Poland's soldiers continued to fight for the defeat of Germany. In the West, after their contribution to the liberation of Holland, they crossed the Rhine into Germany itself.

For four days, the Polish 1st Armoured Division fought fierce battles around the Kusten Canal with the ultimate objective of seizing the port of Wilhelmshaven. An attack began on the defences of the city but it quickly ended. On May 5, 1945, the Germans gave up further resistance and Colonel Antoni Grudzinski received the surrender of the Wilhelmshaven garrison. This turned out to be the last of the many battles fought by the Polish 1st Armoured Division.

Germany fell under Allied occupation and the division was assigned a region south of Wilhelmshaven, around the city of Haren on the Ems River. By this time, it was becoming increasingly clear that Poland itself would not be free. In fact, many of the soldiers from Eastern Poland learned that the land on which their homes had stood would now be handed over directly to the Soviet Union as one of its spoils of war. In this way Poland was made to compensate Russia for the losses it had suffered at the hands of the Germans.

The Polish 1st Armoured Division was dissolved in March 1947. A few of its soldiers elected to return to Poland, whatever its plight, but the majority set sail for Britain, from which they scattered to the four corners of the world.

232

Tanks of the Polish 1st Armoured Division enter the town of Wilhelmshaven.

Papenburg, April 1945. A flame thrower in action.

"The British and Canadian Armies have begun to move into the newly surrendered areas of Denmark, Germany and Holland.... the Polish Armoured is in Wilhelmshaven and to the north, while the Canadian 2nd Infantry Division is spreading between Oldenburg and the left bank of the Wesser."

Correspondent of *The Times* on the occupation of Wilhelmshaven by the Polish 1st Armoured Division. May 7, 1945

■ ■ ■

"The Polish Armoured with the Canadian First Army has made the best advance in the north. Having got over both the Kusten Canal and the River Ems, they took Aschendorf in the face of strong resistance and went on to capture the important centre of Papenburg.

Tonight we learn that they are at a village called Inhrove and on a railway which runs up to Emden, and Papenburg is seven miles behind them."

Correspondent of *The Times* on the fighting of the Polish 1st Armoured Division on German soil. April 22, 1945

On May 5, 1945, the commander of the Polish 1st Armoured Division, Colonel Antoni Grudzinski, together with his officers, accepts the surrender of the town and harbour of Wilhelmshaven.

Eastern Front

General Stanislaw Poplawski, commander of the Polish 1st Army, with Soviet staff members, April 14, 1945

On the eastern front, events were strictly controlled by the Soviet authorities. When the Red Army entered what had been Polish territory, Polish Communists carrying out Soviet Premier Josef Stalin's directives announced universal conscription and began gathering new troops. As a result, two new Polish army groups were formed — the First and the Second Polish People's Armies. Both of these units fought alongside the Red Army as it drove the Germans out of Poland and Czechoslovakia. By the time they approached Germany, their strength had grown to 200,000 men.

During the final phase of the war, the First Polish People's Army advanced on Berlin from the north, while the Second Polish People's Army approached from the southern flank. After encountering strong German resistance, Polish units entered the German capital on May 6, 1945.

They took part in the last engagements in Berlin, fighting in the Tiergarten sector of the city. Among them was the "Kosciuszko" Polish 1st Infantry Division, the first of the Polish units that had been created under direct Soviet control.

Given the fact that the war had started with the German invasion of Poland, in the end it was only fitting that, apart from the Soviet Army itself, the Polish People's Army was the only Allied fighting force that participated directly in the capture of Berlin.

Berlin, May 1945. Soldiers from the Polish People's Army celebrate the victory over Germany.

Berlin, May 1945. Polish artillery passes the Brandenburg Gate.

The Big Three Conference, February 1945. Sitting from left: British Prime Minister Winston Churchill, U.S. President Franklin D. Roosevelt and Soviet Premier Josef Stalin. They met on the grounds of Livadia Palace, Yalta, where the conference was held. *IWM - NAM.237*

Epilogue

....But the Poles, whose death-toll was the greatest of all, had to mourn without comfort or consolation....

Norman Davies in *Heart Of Europe — A Short History Of Poland*

Warsaw, winter 1945. The wreckage of buildings shattered by bombs stand like skeletons. In the final stage of the war, ninety-five per cent of the city was destroyed.

"As the news of the city's condition began to drift slowly through the news channels, the world could only pause in amazement at the thoroughness of war's devastation. This great European city had enjoyed a population of 1,289,000 on 1 January, 1939. It had surrendered on 27 September, 1939, after a heroic resistance of twenty days. For five years and four month it had been ruled by Hitler's lieutenants. It had suffered aerial and land bombardment so intense that hardly a building in the whole city remained undamaged. Latterly it had been ravished by a bitter and bloody revolt. Its population in January 1945 was approximately 25,000."

Brian Gardner in *The Wasted Hour, The Tragedy Of 1945*

Poland had suffered appallingly under the Nazis. More than six million of her citizens — half of them Jews — were killed during the course of the war. The people of entire villages were locked in their churches, which were then set on fire. Thousands of prisoners-of-war were shot or buried alive. Millions more were shipped off to Germany as slave labourers, where many died of hunger, disease and beatings. About 200,000 Polish children were taken to Germany for adoption and only 30,000 returned to Poland to be reunited with their families.

On a per capita basis, Poland suffered the most of any country fighting against Nazi Germany. For every 1,000 of its citizens, 220 died as a result of the war. The next most heavily damaged country, the Soviet Union, suffered 124 dead per 1,000, just over half the Polish rate. Compared to the destruction in Poland, death rates among the other major western Allies were negligible: 13 per 1,000 in France, 8 per 1,000 in Britain, and only 1.4 per 1,000 in the United States.

As of July 1, 1945, two months after the end of the war in Europe, a total of 228,000 Poles were under arms in the West. Of these, 202,000 were in the Army, 3,720 in the Navy, 13,480 in the Air Force, and 5,350 in the Women's Auxiliary. These Armed Forces suffered a total of 21,308 killed, about two-thirds of them in action.

On the Eastern Front, there were about 200,000 Poles in the Polish 1st and 2nd People's Armies. Their casualties reached 27,000 just for the campaign to capture Berlin.

BATTLES	DATE	SOLDIERS	CASUALTIES
POLAND Polish campaign	Sept. 1 - Oct. 5, 1939	800,000	c. 200,000
Polish People's Army in the Battle on Vistula	Aug. 1 - Oct. 3, 1944	65,000	6,900
Warsaw Uprising	Aug.1 - Oct. 2,1944	50,000	18,000
Polish People's Army in the Battle to liberate Poland	Jan. - March 1945	200,000	20,800
FRANCE French campaign	June 10 - June 25, 1940	36,000	6,000
Battle of Falaise (Normandy)	Aug. 14 - Aug. 21, 1944	15,500	2,300
NORWAY Battle of Narvik	May 7 - May 25, 1940	4,500	200
ITALY Battle of Monte Cassino - Piedimonte	May 11 - May 25, 1944	46,000	4,200
Battle of Ancona	June 15 - July 24, 1944	43,000	2,400
AFRICA Battle of Tobruk and El Gazala	Aug. 1941 - April 1942	5,000	635
RUSSIA Battle of Lenino	Oct. 12 - Oct. 13, 1944	12,000	2,000
GERMANY Polish People's Army in the Battle of Berlin	April 16 - May 8, 1945	180,000	27,000

Table from *Za Wolnosc i Lud*

Warsaw, October 1945. Traffic is directed by a Polish army girl.

After five years and eight months of war in which Poland had played an active part from the first day to the last, the country emerged as the biggest loser on the winning side. In 1941, the Polish people were addressed by U.S. President Franklin D. Roosevelt as "an inspiration of nations." At the Tehran conference three years later, Roosevelt agreed to hand Poland over to Soviet rule. The Yalta conference confirmed this American and British betrayal of their Polish ally. In February 1945, Polish soldiers learned that almost half the territory of Poland was to be incorporated directly into the Soviet Union, while the other half was to submit to a government controlled by Moscow. It seemed that the Poles had fought in vain. They were left with nothing but their honour. And those in the West dared not go back to a country wracked by Soviet-style purges.

For Poland and her people, the end of the war in Europe was not met with victory and joy to be followed by peaceful reconstruction. Instead, VE Day ushered in another brutal foreign occupation.

In Moscow on July 26, 1944, representatives of a new pro-Russian Polish government signed an agreement regarding a campaign of repression against the Polish underground movement, members of the Home Army, and those participating in any opposition to the Communist Party. Even though the Home Army had been dissolved in January 1945, more than 10,000 of its members were sent to Soviet prisons and labour camps from October 1944 to May 1945. What was worse, 150,000 were sentenced to death by special military courts. The same fate met Polish soldiers returning to Poland from exile abroad. Altogether, about 105,000 Polish solders were repatriated from Britain to Poland. Those who had covered themselves in glory at the battles of Narvik, Monte Cassino, Tobruk, and Falaise were arrested on charges of spying, killing Soviet soldiers and collaborating with Hitler. Exactly how many vanished during the years from 1945 to 1957 will never be known.

Many Poles refused to recognize the new authorities imposed on them by the Soviets. Active resistance lasted for some years after the end of the Second World War, and if one looks at the regular eruptions of popular protest that punctuated Polish post-war history — 1956, 1968, 1970, 1976 and 1980 — one can say that resistance to Soviet rule never really ended. It only ceased when the Communist regime itself collapsed in 1989 and Poland once again tasted independence.

242

"It is, indeed, a mournful reflection that this Empire, which stood alone in 1940, except for Poland, against the might of triumphant Nazi Germany, cannot now, when she has mighty Allies by her side, stand up for juster treatment of her first and most martyred Ally of this war. But if, indeed, it be so, let us at least comport ourselves with dignity and honour. Do not let us pretend that something which is unjust is in reality right. Do not turn away from our own shores those who have given their lifeblood for the protection of our homes."

Captain Alan Graham's speech in the House of Commons during debate on the Crimea Conference. February 27, 1945

"I feel sure that the House would wish me to pay a tribute to the magnificent services which these forces of one of our first Allies in the late war have rendered to the common cause throughout the whole long struggle. His Majesty's Government and, I am sure, the whole House, are conscious of their debt to these men. It is a matter of profound regret to me that some hon. Friends in this House have coupled the existence of these forces with the relationships of ourselves and the U.S.S.R. I think no greater injustice has been done to a body of men than to make these brilliant soldiers the subject of propaganda on either side."

Secretary of State for Foreign Affairs Ernest Bevin's statement on the problem of Polish Armed Forces under British command, in the House of Commons. March 20, 1946

"We have immense sympathy for that very valorous, brave Ally, who have fought the Boche for five years inside and outside their own country, a country which has always maintained its national consciousness through four partitions....
I have heard it said that the Poles are a difficult people. Perhaps they are. So should we be, if half our country were to be given away to somebody else. The Poles have no monopoly of being difficult in the world today. But the Poles have not been conquered. They are still fighting. They are fighting in the underground movement. This is not a case of *vae victis*. We know perfectly well that when a country has been defeated, she must bear the consequences. She may have to bear the most dreadful horrible consequences but that is because she lost the war. In this case Poland has not lost the war, she is our Ally, she is our continuing Ally and she is fighting by our side."

M. Petherick's speech in the House of Commons, moving an amendment to a motion of the Prime Minister during debate on the Crimea Conference. February 28, 1945

Warsaw, the heroic city that refused to die. The capital of Poland was almost erased from the map, for such was the Germans' purpose. Despite destruction like this of the Three Crosses Church, the Poles decided to pitch in with all their energies to rebuild the city.

Lech Walesa, leader of the Solidarity movement, during the strike in the Gdansk Shipyard, August 1980. *Polish Interpress Agency*

During the years following the Yalta agreement, a new generation of Poles was raised in silence. Teachers taught that the Red Army was the only power, that the only war heroes were those fighting on the Soviet front, that the only underground resistance in Poland to German occupation was led by the Communist Party and the Polish People's Army. No mention was ever made of the thousands who lost their lives on the western front, or during the Soviet invasion of Eastern Poland in September 1939, or at the hands of the NKVD in the Katyn forest, or in the Warsaw Uprising while Soviet troops stood idly on the other side of the Vistula.

During the darkest days of Stalinist oppression, even correspondence with the Polish emigré community in the West was regarded as treason, even if that correspondence was with a relative or friend.

Despite intense repression, the Polish spirit was still alive. Poles did not forget the crimes committed by the Soviets against their country. Hatred for all things Soviet continued unabated, erupting in violent protests in 1956, 1968, 1970 and 1976. Finally, with the birth of the Solidarity movement in 1980, what had hitherto been sporadic became one mass ongoing campaign of unrelenting resistance. Refusing to be cowed by the declaration of martial law in 1981, the Polish people continued their pressure. It was this more than any other single factor that contributed to the overthrow of the entire Soviet imperial system by the end of the 1980s.

245

Sikorski Museum

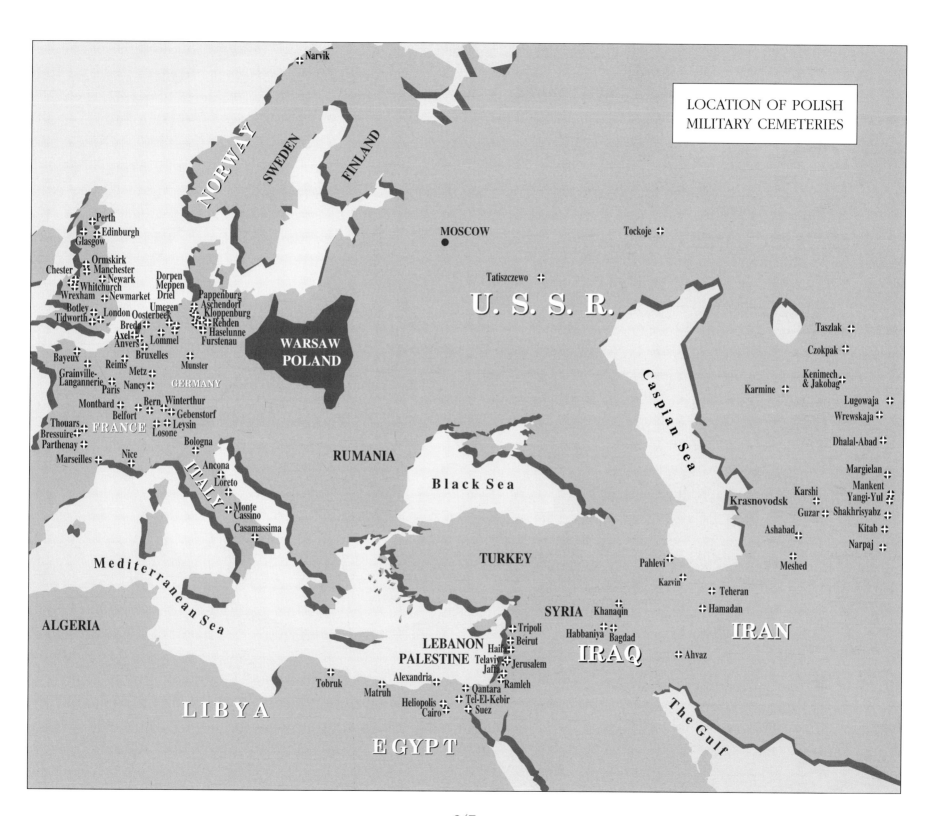

LOCATION OF POLISH
MILITARY CEMETERIES

Narvik

NORWAY
SWEDEN
FINLAND

MOSCOW

Tockoje

Perth
Edinburgh
Glasgow

Ormskirk
Chester
Manchester
Newark
Whitchurch
Wrexham
Newmarket
Botley
London Oosterbeek
Tidworth
Breda
Axel
Anvers
Lommel
Bayeux
Bruxelles
Reims
Metz
Munster
Grainville-
Langannerie
Paris Nancy
GERMANY
Montbard
Bern Winterthur
Belfort
Gebenstorf
Thouars
Leysin
Bressuire
Losone
Parthenay
Bologna
Marseilles
Nice
Ancona

Dorpen
Meppen
Driel
Pappenburg
Aschendorf
Umegen
Kloppenburg
Rehden
Haselunne
Furstenau

WARSAW
POLAND

U. S. S. R.

Tatiszczewo

Taszlak

Czokpak

Kenimech
& Jakobag

Karmine

Lugowaja

Wrewskaja

Dhalal-Abad

Caspian Sea

Margielan

Mankent
Yangi-Yul

Karshi

Shakhrisyabz

Guzar

Kitab

Ashabad

Narpaj

Krasnovodsk

FRANCE
ITALY
Loreto
Monte
Cassino
Casamassima

RUMANIA

Black Sea

Meshed

TURKEY

Pahlevi

Kazvin

Teheran

Hamadan

IRAN

Ahvaz

Mediterranean Sea

ALGERIA

SYRIA
Khanaqin

Habbaniya
Bagdad

IRAQ

LIBYA

Tobruk

Matruh

LEBANON
PALESTINE
Haifa
Telaviv
Jaffa
Jerusalem
Tripoli
Beirut

Alexandria

Heliopolis
Cairo

Ramleh
Qantara
Tel-El-Kebir
Suez

The Gulf

EGYPT

247

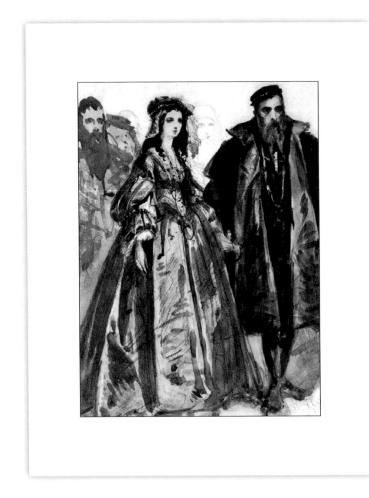

A Short History of Poland

Polonia, or Poland, called by the Natives Polska, takes its name from Pole, which in the Slavian language (here commonly spoken) signifies a plain and champaign Country, such as this Kingdom for the most part consists of. Other suppose, that the inhabitants, from their first Captain Lechus or Lachus, being called Po-lachi, and by corruption Polani and Poloni imparted their name to the country.

The Kingdom is bounden on the North by the Baltic Sea, and the Swedish Livonia. On the East by the Muscovian Russia. On the South by Moldavia, Transylvania and Hungary from which the Nister and the high and woody Carpathian mountains divide it. On the West by Silesia, the Marquisate of Brandenburg, and the further Pomerane.

The people of Poland are the undoubted offspring of the Slavi, Slavini, or Slavonias, seated on the north-side of the Carpathian mountains.

The Polanders are generally of a good complexion, flaxen-hair'd, and tall of stature. The men for the most part, corpulent and personable. The women, slender and beautiful, disdaining the help of art and focus's to set them off.

They are naturally open-hearted and candid; more apt to be deceived, than to deceive; not so easily provoked as appeas'd; neither arrogant, nor obstinate; but very tractable if they be gently and prudently managed.

The Gentlemen (who are all noble) take delight in keeping great store of Horses and Arms.

The chief strength of Poland consists in their Cavalry which is very numerous and readily raised; the nobility being bound by the Laws of the Land, to attend the King in all expeditions for the security of the Kingdom.... But these forces, when assembled, serve only for the defence of their country, and as they are composed principally of the Nobles, they frequently signalize themselves by their valour, and successes against the much grater number of their enemies.

Thus Zamoschius is the time of Sigismund the third with 3000 men worsted Carigereius the Scythian who, with 7000, was making an inroad into Poland, and forced him with a lot of many thousands of his Tatars to return into his own country Taurica Chersonesus. And Zolkievi with 3000 horse, setting upon 80000 Muscovites unawares, put themselves all to fight: and brought away prisoners three German Regiments that served amongst them.

Sections from *The English Atlas*

250

*T*he Polish state emerged in the second half of the tenth century and grew into an imposing kingdom. At its peak in the fifteenth and sixteenth centuries, the Polish kingdom stretched between the Baltic and the Black seas. It was a constitutional monarchy, bound by a rich legal tradition and ruled by a king who was elected for life by an assembly of all the nobility. It was also a multicultural commonwealth in which Poles, Lithuanians, Ukrainians, Germans, Jews and a host of other nationalities co-existed, each with its own rights and privileges. Lying athwart major trade routes, the Polish Commonwealth engaged in extensive commercial relations, supplying Western Europe with grain as well as the materials of shipping — timber, hemp (for rope), flax (for sailcloth) and pitch (for caulking).

Poland's geography, however, left it exposed on all sides. From the east, it was continuously raided by Tatars. Later, the growing power of Moscow challenged its hold on Ukraine and Byelorussia. In the south, having swept through the Balkans, the Ottoman Turks faced Poland at what had once been the Hungarian frontier. In the north, the Swedes sought to turn the Baltic Sea into their own lake. And on its western side, what had once been the frontier duchy of Brandenburg emerged as an increasingly militaristic and aggressive Prussia.

Beset on all sides, Poland did not have internal institutions that were equal to the task of preserving independence. In a misguided attempt at protecting minority rights, the Polish nobility asserted the *liberum veto* — the right of any representative in parliament to block legislation and dissolve the session. From 1652 onward, the veto was used to paralyze government. Poland's neighbours quickly learned that they could bring opposition to a standstill by suborning a few unscrupulous individuals, and so the Polish Commonwealth fell into decline.

By the end of the eighteenth century, Poland's internal paralysis contrasted dramatically with the aggressive expansionism of its neighbours, Russia, Prussia and Austria. In 1772, in what came to be known as the first partition of Poland, these three Empires helped themselves to large stretches of Polish territory.

First Partition, 1772   Second Partition, 1793   Third Partition, 1795

This first partition shocked the nation out of its lethargy. A vigorous reform effort was launched. Poland created the world's first national ministry of education to oversee a cultural rebirth. A new military academy was founded to train professional soldiers. And the process was capped by the proclamation of a new constitution on May 3, 1791. As a result, social relationships were reformed, the franchise was extended, and Poland became only the second state in the world (after the United States) to be governed by a written constitutional document.

All of this, however, was in vain. Incensed by Polish efforts to strengthen their state, Russia and Prussia engineered a second partition of the country in 1793. Poles rose up in resistance. On June 4, 1794, at Raclawice, Tadeusz Kosciuszko led a poorly equipped army of nobles and farmers to victory against a larger and better equipped Russian army. Despite this short-lived triumph, Warsaw fell to Russian and Prussian forces. Typically, General Aleksander W. Suvorov's Russian Army slaughtered 12,000 men, women and children upon entering the city.

The third partition of Poland divided up the remaining territories of Poland among Russia, Prussia and Austria. A state that had existed for 800 years was erased from the map of Europe.

The partitions of Poland marked the end of the old Commonwealth, but they ushered in a new era of revolutionary struggle. The next century of Polish history was marked by an unrelenting campaign to regain national independence.

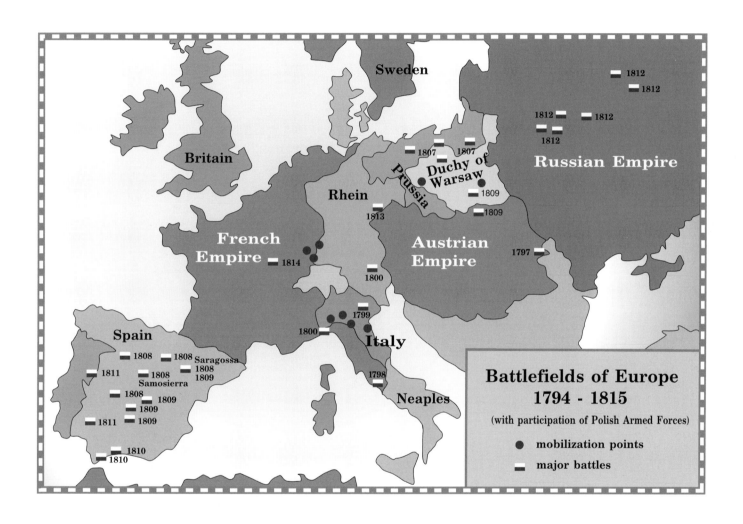

Battlefields of Europe 1794 - 1815

(with participation of Polish Armed Forces)

● mobilization points

▬ major battles

Seeing a chance for their country through an alliance with revolutionary France, Polish armies attached themselves to Napoleon's rising star. Under the motto "For Your Freedom and Ours," Polish armies fought with Napoleon's forces in Italy and in Germany. For their efforts, they were rewarded with the small Duchy of Warsaw, which depended entirely on Napoleon's favour and disappeared with the failure of the French invasion of Russia in 1812.

After the Napoleonic Wars, 1815

The 1815 Congress of Vienna, which defined the shape of post-Napoleonic Europe, engineered yet another partition of Poland. The Duchy of Warsaw disappeared and Polish territories were reassigned, with the Russian Empire receiving the lion's share. Polish territories under Russian rule were reorganized into a new "kingdom" of Poland that was to be ruled by the Russian Tsar in perpetuity. What little autonomy there was soon eroded as the Russian administration sought to extend Russian laws and strengthen Russian control over this dwarf realm.

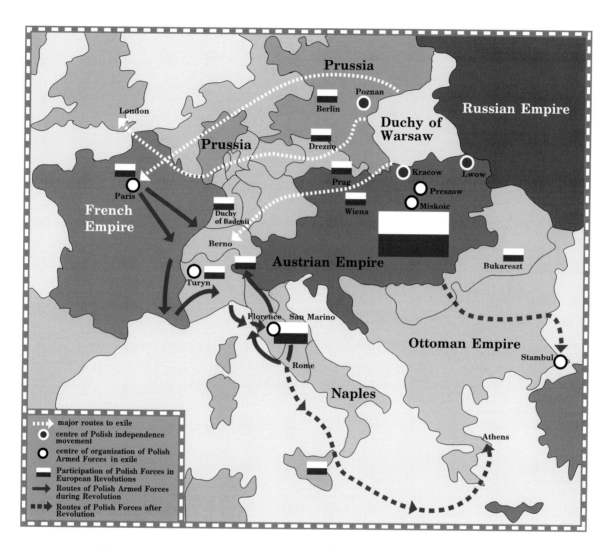

Prussia

Russian Empire

Prussia

Duchy of
Warsaw

London

Berlin

Poznan

Drezno

Kracow

Lwow

French
Empire

Prag

Preszow

Miskoic

Paris

Duchy
of Badenii

Wiena

Berno

Austrian Empire

Bukareszt

Turyn

Florence   San Marino

Ottoman Empire

Rome

Stambul

Naples

Athens

major routes to exile

centre of Polish independence
movement

centre of organization of Polish
Armed Forces in exile

Participation of Polish Forces in
European Revolutions

Routes of Polish Armed Forces
during Revolution

Routes of Polish Forces after
Revolution

From 1846 to 1848, revolutionary and nationalistic movements known as the Spring
of Nations swept throughout Europe. Poles played important roles in many, fighting
"For Your Freedom and Ours" in Sicily, Baden, France, Saxony, Hungary and Belgium.

255

The history of the nineteenth century is punctuated by two uprisings against Russian rule, one in 1830 and the other in 1863. On both occasions, despite ferocious resistance by the Poles, the numerical superiority of the Russians prevailed. With the collapse of each insurrection, institutions were closed, property was confiscated, and tens of thousands of patriots were either executed or deported to Siberia. Even the public use of the Polish language was forbidden.

Despite repression, Poland's spirit remained strong. Many Polish artists went into exile. Paris became the centre of their political and cultural activities and the works of these emigrés was smuggled back into the country where it was read, performed surreptitiously and taught in underground schools and universities.

A new generation of patriots was brought up in the spirit of hope for a free and an independent Poland.

The First World War

Parade of Independence. Warsaw, November 11, 1918

The First World War brought new hope for the Polish people. Europe was divided by the bloodiest conflict in history. Russia found itself allied with Great Britain and France against Germany and Austria. As a result, much of the fighting in the East between Russia and Germany took place over Polish land. The bewildered Poles were conscripted into the armies of both sides. While some fought in the Tsar's armies, their brothers fought for the Austro-Hungarian Emperor and the German Kaiser.

There were, however, other Poles, especially those in exile in Western Europe, who saw the war as a tremendous opportunity to redress the wrongs done to Poland and redraw the map of Europe. They campaigned tirelessly for an independent Poland. When it became clear that the three empires that had once partitioned Poland were all collapsing under the weight of war, the Polish case for independence became unstoppable. It was enshrined as one of American President Woodrow Wilson's famous Fourteen Points for the conclusion of the war.

When the war did come to an end, a revived Polish state arose out of the ashes.

Polish independence was proclaimed in Warsaw on November 11, 1918, and was confirmed by the Treaty of Versailles on June 28, 1919.

Marshal Jozef Pilsudski, great soldier, politician, statesman of Poland. He declared Poland as independent republic in 1918. As prime minister of Poland, Pilsudski foresaw the expansion of Stalinizm on one side and Hitler on the other. He formulated the doctrine of "Two Enemies."

Before the devastation of war

could be addressed, the new state had to fight to preserve its new-found freedom. The Russian monarchy had been swept away by the Bolsheviks.

In 1920, Russia's revolutionary leadership declared: "The road to the world revolution leads over the dead body of Poland."

Once again, Russian armies closed in on Warsaw. In the south, a counterattack was being prepared by Polish Marshal Jozef Pilsudski and Wladyslaw Sikorski, future leader of Poland's forces in the Second World War. Just when all seemed lost, the Polish 5th and 3rd Armies drove north in a surprise attack that cut off the Russian advance. The Polish victory was as surprising as it was overwhelming. To this day, Poles refer to it as the "miracle" on the Vistula. As a result, Polish independence was preserved, and the Bolsheviks failed to gain their much-hoped-for springboard from which to launch revolutions into the heart of Europe.

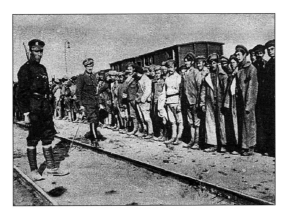

Polish volunteers for the war against Bolshevik Russia.

"The influence of this decisive battle on history was fully appreciated by Tukhachevski, who lost it, and by Lord D'Abernon, who watched it. Yet, strange to say, its importance was little grasped by Western Europe, and since has remained little noticed. Soon after his defeat Tukhachevski wrote:

> 'In all European countries Capitalism was staggering; the workers were lifting their heads and rushing to arms. There is not the slightest doubt that, had we been victorious on the Vistula, the revolution would have set light to the entire continent of Europe.... Exported revolution is possible... and had it not been for our strategic mistakes and our defeat on the Field of Battle, perhaps the Polish war would have been the link which would have initiated the revolution of October to the revolution of Western Europe.... There cannot be the slightest doubt that had we succeeded in disrupting the Polish Army of bourgeois and lords, the revolution of the Polish class workers would have been a *fait accompli*, and the conflagration would not have halted on the Polish frontiers. Like an overwhelming torrent it would have swept into Western Europe. The Red Army will never forget this experiment in exported revolution, and if ever the bourgeoisie of Europe invites us to new struggles, the Red Army will succeed in destroying it and fomenting revolution in Europe'."

Major General J.F.C. Fuller in *The Decisive Battles Of The Western World*

"The history of contemporary civilization knows no event of greater importance than the Battle of Warsaw, 1920, and none of which the significance is less appreciated. The danger menacing Europe at that moment was parried, and the whole episode forgotten. Had the battle been a Bolshevik victory, it would have been a turning point in European history, for there is no doubt at all that the whole of Central Europe would at that moment have been opened to the influence of Communist propaganda and a Soviet invasion, which it could with difficulty have resisted....

The events of 1920 also deserve attention for another reason: victory was obtained, above all, thanks to the strategical genius of one man and thanks to the carrying through of maneuvers so dangerous as to necessitate not only genius, but heroism....

It should be the task of political writers to explain to European opinion that Poland saved Europe in 1920, and that it is necessary to keep Poland powerful and in harmonious relations with Western European civilization, for Poland is the barrier to the everlasting peril of an Asiatic invasion."

Further, by shielding Central Europe from the full blast of Marxist contagion, the Battle of Warsaw set back the Bolshevik clock. It deprived Russia of the plunder she badly needed to stem her desperate economic crisis and dammed the outward flow of discontent and almost drowned the Bolshevik experiment.

This was the 18th decisive battle in world history."

Lord D'Abernon in *Gazeta Polska* about the Battle of Warsaw, London, August 17, 1930

General Wladyslaw Sikorski, commander of the Northern Polish Army, questions deserters from the Red Army.

The Pole, though he is famed in all the nations of the earth,
For loving more than life itself the country of his birth,
Yet he is ready to depart and to the world's end go,
And live the weary length of years in misery and woe,
Fighting against the might of men and destiny's cruel hand,
That through the storm his hope may shine:
I serve my fatherland.

Adam Mickiewicz from *Pan Tadeusz*, 1834

Bibliography

Baluk, Stefan S. *Poles On The Fronts Of World War II*. Warsaw: ARS Print Production, 1995.

Bielatowicz, Jan. *Ramie Pancerne 2 Polskiego Korpusu: Album Fotografii 2 Warszawskiej Dywizji Pancernej*. Rzym: Referat Kultury i Prasy 2 Warszawskiej Dywizji Pancernej, 1946.

Collins, James L. *Encyclopedia Of World War II*. New York: Marshal Cavendish Corporation, 1972.

Curtis, Rosmé. *Winged Tenacity*. England, 1944.

Davies, Norman. *Heart Of Europe: A Short History of Poland*. New York: Oxford University Press, 1984.

Divine, A.D. *Dunkirk*. London: Faber & Faber Ltd., 1945.

Divine, A.D. *Navies In Exile*. London: J.Murray, 1944.

Fargo, Ladislas. *The Game Of The Foxes: The Untold Story Of German Espionage In The United States And Great Britain During World War II*. New York: David McKay Company, 1972.

Fuller, J.F.C. *The Decisive Battles Of The Western World And Their Influence Upon History*. Volume 3. London: Eyre & Spottiswoode, 1957.

Felsztyn, Tadeusz. *Dzieje 2 Korpusu*. Londyn: Gryf, 1947.

Filipow, Krzysztof. Wawer Zbigniew. *Passerby, Tell Poland... Narvik, Tobruk, Monte Cassino, Falaise*. Warszawa: Wydawnictwo Arkady, 1991.

Gilbert, Martin. *The Churchill War Papers*, Volume 1, *At the Admirality*. New York, London: W.W. Norton & Company, 1993.

Gilbert, Martin. *The Churchill War Papers*, Volume 2, *Never Surrender*. London: Heineman, 1993.

Holman, Gordon. *The Little Ships*. London: Hodder & Stoughton, 1943.

Jewsiewicki, Wladyslaw. *Powstanie Warszawskie 1944: Okiem Polskiej Kamery*. Warszawa: Wydawnictwo Interpress, 1989.

Johnson, Brian. *The Secret War*. London: British Broadcasting Corporation, 1978.

Kleczkowski, Stefan. *Poland's First 100,000: The Story Of The Rebirth Of The Polish Army, Navy And Air Force After The September Campaign, Together With A Biographical Note About Its Creator General Sikorski*. London: Hutchinson & Co. Ltd., 1946.

Kopf, Stanislaw. *Lata Okupacji — Kronika Forograficzna Walczacej Warszawy*. Warszawa: Instytut Wydawniczy PAX, 1989.

Kosianowski, Wladyslaw. *Polska Marynarka Wojenna: Od Pierwszej Do Ostatniej Salwy W Drugiej Wojnie Swiatowej*, Album Pamiatkowy. Rzym: Instytur Literacki, 1947.

Kozlowski, Eugeniusz. *Wojna Obronna Polski 1939*. Warszawa: Wydawnictwo Obronny Narodowej, 1979.

Krolikowski, Lucjan. *Stolen Childhood: A Saga Of Polish War Children*. New York: Father Justin Rosary Hour, Buffalo, 1983.

Laitgeber, Witold, *It Speaks For Itself: What British War Leaders Said About The Polish Armed Forces*. London: Polish Forces Press Bureau, 1946.

Marley, David. *The Daily Telegraph: Story Of The War*. London: Hodder & Stoughton Limited Publishers, 1942.

Onoszko, Aleksander. *Mimo Wszystko Latac*. Warszawa: Wydawnictwo Altair, 1993.

Ostrowski, Wiktor. *Zolnierz Z Monte Cassino: Album Fotograficzny Z Terenu I Okresu Bitwy*. Rzym,: Oddzial Kultury i Prasy 2-go Korpusu A.P., 1945.

Poznanski, Stanislaw. *Struggle, Death, Memory: On The Twentieth Anniversary Of The Rising In The Warsaw Ghetto*. Poland: Artistic and Film Publications, State Enterprise, 1943.

Romanska, Lola, and Romanski, Andrzej. *In Their Country Service: Women — Soldiers Of The 2nd Polish Corps, 1941-1946*. Rome: Headquarters Of The Polish Women's Auxiliary Corps, Polish 2nd Corps, 1946.

Rutkowski, Adam. *Meczenstwo, Walka, Zaglada Zydow W Polsce 1939-1945*. Warszawa: Wydawnictwo Ministerstwa Obrony Narodowej, 1960.

Saywell, Shelley. *Women In War: First Hand Accounts From World War II to El Salvador*. New York: Viking, 1985.

Sereny, Gitta. *Albert Speer: His Battle With Truth*. New York: Alfred A. Knopf, 1995.

Stevenson, William. *A Man Called Interepid: The Secret War*. New York, London: Harcourt Brace Jovanovich, 1993.

Waller, John H. *The Unseen War In Europe: Espionage And Conspiracy In The Second World War*. New York: Random House, 1996.

Wankowicz, Melchior. *Bitwa O Monte Cassino*. Rzym: Wydawnictwo Kultury i Prasy Drugiego Polskiego Korpusu, 1945.

Welchman, Gordon. *The Hut Six Story — Breaking The Enigma Codes*. New York: McGraw-Hill Book Company, 1982.

Wysocki, Tadeusz A. *1 Polska Dywizja Pancerna 1938-1947*. Londyn: Polska Fundacja Kulturalna, 1989.

Destiny Can Wait: The Polish Air Force In The Second World War. London, William Heinemann Ltd., 1949.

The English Atlas. Volume I. Oxford: Sansonius a Waesberge, and Steven Swart, Booksellers in Amsterdam, MDCLXXX.

Za Nasza I Wasza Wolnosc. New York: Polish Information Center, 1941.

Za Wolnosc I Lud. Issue 7. Warsaw: 1-15 April 1965.

Parliamentary statements and reports: *Hansard: Parliamentary Reports*. London.

Air Ministry and Admirality communiques, statements and messages and various other official sources: *It Speaks For Itself: What British War Leaders Said About The Polish Armed Forces* by Letigeber W.

Index